The Journey Home: How to be Church

Phyllis Calvey

Illustrations by
Brian Calvey

Sheed & Ward

Sheed & Ward™ is a service of The National Catholic Reporter Publishing Company.

Library of Congress Cataloguing in Publication Data

Calvey, Phyllis
ISBN: 1-55612-702-2

Published by: Sheed & Ward
                  115 E. Armour Blvd.
                  P.O. Box 419492
                  Kansas City, MO 64141

To order, call: (800) 333-7373

Contents

Dedication

To Rev. James Connolly
> ". . . The glory of children are their fathers."
>
> Proverbs 17:6

We see the world through the windows of the houses in which we grew up. Our families become an expression of the view we were given. We see God through the windows of our churches. And our communities, too, become an expression of that view. If we have a childlike joy that colors our community, an easy relationship with God that is based on love and not fear, if we are servant to one another, and see every child of God as our sister and brother, it is simply because we have been given that view of the Kingdom by "our Father," James Connolly.

Acknowledgments

Seventeen years ago I began my journey home. In a church that had all the warmth of my mother's kitchen, the combination of community, Scripture and Father's inspired homilies proved to be the yeast that would awaken new life within my soul, something for which I had long prayed. When I was ready to rise out of myself, our family enrolled in the adult religious education program. We took part in the exciting liturgies, Holy Week, and Penitentials that were creatively and prayerfully presented to our parish. We joined Bible study. How easy it was to grow within the arms of such a supportive church family. A strong lay leadership had already prepared the places I needed to continue on my journey, a faith journey that would eventually lead to my role as Pastoral Associate. I begin by rightfully acknowledging those who paved the road before me.

As I grew in the family, Father Connolly sensed I was ready to begin assuming responsibility. He gently encouraged me to return my gifts to the Lord, always treating me as an equal, always opening the door to new ministry that would finally evolve into the full time position I now hold.

I have learned so much from my qualified colleagues who are loving friends as well, Gerry Perreault, the DRE, and Rita Pizzi, our Youth Minister. We look out of the same windows of the House of the Lord, yet we each see a different view. This is our strength, bringing our unique visions, talents, and expertise to the community. Our positions are an integral part of the development of the parish as a whole.

Each member of the community is in some way part of the writing of this book. However, I would like to thank the people who wrote something specifically. Gerry Perreault. Rita Pizzi. Maureen Britton. Kim Carney. Michael Murzycki. Beth Taub. Jacque Martino. Scott Britton. Miki Loumos. Carolyn Carey. Jackie Farese. Ed Braley. MaryAnn Matejka.

My deepest love to my two children, Trevor and Jessie, who have shown me the difference church can make in a family.

I am particularly grateful to Don and Rose Calvey for all their love and support. Our dearest friends, Mary Pat and Mike Yates. They have tirelessly listened to my ideas, critiqued my work, celebrated and supported my writing for many years. To my Serendipity people for the sharing of the "Upper Room." To my sister Debbie whose goodness was the result of my first published story. To Barbara Fouhy who has truly been a Godsend, relieving me of office work at a time when I was overwhelmed. To Millie Woodman for taking care of us. I could never thank Joe Coley enough for providing a computer, and patiently being there every time I needed him. It never ceases to amaze me how this family so freely shares with one another. And I find my fulfillment comes directly out of the love we have found together as community.

As I sat for hours at my desk writing about this church family, I experienced the intimacy of our relationship that is based in Jesus; an intimacy of button friends and kindred spirits. The community has become my family in the true Biblical sense. The tithe from this book will be given in the name of the St. Blaise Community.

There are many "family" stories that remain untold. Robert Heyer, the editor of Sheed and Ward, recognized and drew this story of our community out of my heart. My conversations with him and Andy Apathy, the Production Manager, set a fire within me that burned to speak of the Church Jesus gave to believers, the channel where we would be empowered to live the Gospel message. There is no coincidence with God. He chose these Christian hands to mold my work for the Kingdom. It is strange how we have to fill out the necessary worldly contracts. Yet, there is between us the silent understanding of the Covenant we are all bound to—the new Covenant that binds our living to the higher laws that have been written by God upon our hearts.

I end with a grateful heart to my parents, Phil and Yvonne Vadenais, who gave me my relationship with Jesus by deciding to make church part of our lives. They gave me the foundation of my faith, the feeling of Sunday that made me long to journey home . . .

from Phyllis and Brian Calvey
two who love God joined as one

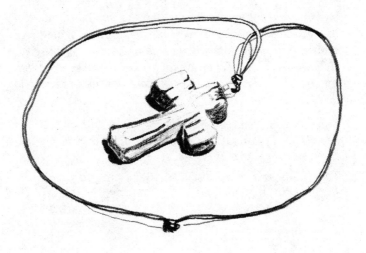

Introduction

Jesus Calms a Storm

On the evening of that same day Jesus said to his disciples, "Let us go across to the other side of the lake." So they left the crowd; the disciples got into the boat in which Jesus was already sitting, and they took him with them. Other boats were there too. Suddenly a strong wind blew up, and the waves began to spill over into the boat, so that it was about to fill with water. Jesus was in the back of the boat, sleeping with his head on a pillow. The disciples woke him up and said, "Teacher, don't you care that we are about to die?"

Jesus stood up and commanded the wind, "Be quiet!" and he said to the waves, "Be still!" The wind died down, and there was a great calm.

Then Jesus said to his disciples, "Why are you frightened? Do you still have no faith?"

Mark 4:35-41

❖   ❖   ❖

The Journey Home

They all come home by a different way. Many come back to church through the Sacraments, especially Baptism. Some seek religious education for their school-age children. There are a host of usual channels that have always led people back to the church at different times in their lives.

Many families have shared their pleasant surprise and joy at what they are discovering upon their return. They are coming back to church and finding that people are here because they want to be. There is no longer that feeling of obligation, rather a sense of privilege. They expected that coming home would be difficult since many returned with old wounds that had never quite healed. Instead, they were greeted with the kind of warmth that bestows permission to come home, with no feeling of condition attached to the invitation.

They cannot believe how much they have missed being home. The feeling of Sunday. They do not remember church being so informal or so friendly. But they have their own stories to remember. Stories that for good or bad gave them their relationship with Jesus. This is what they have long wanted for their children, this same chance to know the Lord. And deep down they understood that this could only happen through the experience of church in the family.

They had always wanted to come home, and now they found a reason to stay.

❖   ❖   ❖

Community

> *"He sat down to eat with them, took the bread, and said the blessing; then he broke the bread and gave it to them. Then their eyes were opened and they recognized him ..."*
>
> Luke 24:30-31

It was a good thing Father walked in behind the Bishop. He nearly fell over when he saw the crowd for the 5:00 Mass. The previous Sunday he had announced about the bishop's visitation of the parish, and had jokingly said if we went to the two Masses that weekend we could all skip church the next weekend!

Every face in the church was beaming. The man in the third row who had gathered all his grown children, their spouses and children, and was taking the whole crew out to dinner in ex-

change for their attendance. People had brought in neighbors. There had even been volunteers to flag people in off the street. But perhaps the most touching sight was the 19-year-old crowd who brought in their friends. And leave it up to these young people to think of bringing umbrellas and placing these and their biggest overcoats in the benches to make the church look even more full.

At Sunday Mass the next morning, the bishop joined in the fun. He was quite familiar with people in the parish, and as he greeted them for the second time, he smiled and said heartily, "I feel like we've met before!" The bishop was deeply touched by what he saw. Beneath the smiles, he could see the strength, the joy, and the love of a family who was there for one another. He could see the unmistakable love that was exchanged between each person and Father.

Could church really be as simple as we see it? We are a family. And out of that family certain members assume leadership roles. The family accepts this as being the natural development of family. Father Connolly believes that leadership should arise from within a strong faith community. He relinquishes control as the "children" assume their rightful responsibility within the family. The positions of Pastoral Minister, Director of Religious Education, and Youth Minister were all filled from within the community. This is the case for all of our programs.

Therefore, the Pastoral Minister, Youth Minister, Children's Liturgy people, all the leaders, are part of the parish religious education program, and directly involved in most, if not all of the parish programs. Not because it is part of their job description. Rather, it is part of their own faith development. In this way, they are present to "see" the needs of the community as those needs arise directly out of these shared experiences. In turn, the programs we run change and grow with the community because they are so linked to the lifeline of the community.

All of the people involved in any program are part of the tithing program. Their weekly return gift to the Lord is made within the framework of that particular family. They feel the bond that comes from sacrificing for the family.

Because we all worship in the same community, we experience the needs of the family in the intimacy that comes from "eating" at the same table. Perhaps you have experienced this when you attend a different church for one reason or another. The words are the same. There is a beautiful sense of the larger family of God. But the feeling is totally different. It's the difference of being invited to someone else's house for dinner. This is especially felt during Eucharist. As we share the bread, there is an exchange of love. The faces around the table reflect shared moments. The love experienced between two mothers at playgroup who took care of someone's children, or planned a meal together for a mother who just had a baby. The simple glance of a new Baptism family who is coming to church again because of the connection and warmth they felt the night of the Baptism class. The teenager who whispers something to the Youth Minister on the way up to Communion. The Word becoming flesh, presenting Himself in one another.

There is also the consciousness of the Pastoral Minister noting who isn't there. Planning ways to pastor the people, to draw them back to the House of the Lord. The Director of Religious Education attuned to the homily, observing how the community is being formed through the Gospel message. Continuing this formation and addressing needs and concerns raised in the homily. All our people growing together and depending on one another to respond to the Gospel message. This is especially felt as the envelopes are placed on the altar as part of our prayer, as part of our lives.

For our community, to work and worship in the same place allows us to best meet the needs of our people. Of course, there are problems attached to this. We all have very different personalities. It is harder to pray when there is a problem "at work," since there is no separation between work and church. The closer we become, the more vulnerable we are to hurt. There is more at stake when we have disagreements. Our own harmony with one another affects the community because we work so closely together. It is not easy. But we have reached the point that many families reach. We've gone through too much to not make this work. We also have a strong relationship to draw from and through that relationship have come to realize that what we have is too precious to give up. So we accept our differences, allow for our personalities, struggle, know we will be hurt at times, forgive, and continue to grow stronger because of it.

This too is felt in the sharing of the bread. We gather around the table, one family, sisters and brothers, offering up our different gifts, as well as our differences. We bow our heads for the mealtime blessing. "Take this, all of you, and eat, this is my body which has been given up for you. Do this in memory of me. This is my blood, the blood of the new and everlasting covenant, which is being poured out for you. Whenever you drink it, do so in memory of me."

The family, learning to give in, learning to let go, to gather around the table in memory of what Jesus has asked of us. Liturgy becoming a celebration of what we do in memory of Jesus.

As much as we love our community, we realize there is not one way of doing things, nor is there one perfect church. Many families have left our church. Some people need more definite rules to live by. Having rules to follow gives them a sense of security. People left because of our religious education program. They do not want a family program. They want their children to attend weekly classes. Our church is too informal for many. Too friendly for some. Many people have a problem with Father's vision of a pacifist church. Father has taken a direct stand against war and has opted to pay the price in many ways for his unpopular view. We have found that many families today search for the church that is right for them. Slowly, church becomes the expression of the priest and the people who belong to it.

The following is a beautiful passage from Isaiah, called God's Wisdom. Isaiah was addressing "you arrogant men who rule here in Jerusalem over this people."

> Listen to what I am saying; pay attention to what I am telling you. No farmer goes on constantly plowing his fields and getting them ready for planting. Once he has prepared the soil, he plants rows of wheat and barley, and at the edges of his fields he plants other grain. He knows how to do his work, because God has taught him. He never uses a heavy club to beat out dill seeds or cumin seeds; instead he uses light sticks of the proper size. He does not ruin the wheat by threshing it endlessly, and he knows how to thresh it by driving a cart over it without bruising the grains. All this wisdom comes from the Lord Almighty. The plans God makes are wise, and they always succeed.

Isaiah is quite harsh in his addressing of those words. Yet, there is such a gentleness and message of love in that passage. The hope for the church. The "farmer" represents the leaders of the church. How well the farmer in the passage understands the needs of the people. Never ruining the wheat by threshing it endlessly. Never bruising the grains. But more importantly, knowing when to stop plowing and plant.

This is our story. The story of the priest and the people. Father Connolly being the farmer who knows when to plant. The story of a community who became ready to accept the seeds. This is God's Wisdom, how to be church.

In the early days Father Connolly often spoke to us about community. We had all come home by a different way. Individual believers who were searching for church in their lives. With patience and insight he readied the fields, getting his people ready for planting. And as each "field" became ready he entrusted that person with a seed to sow. Slowly, our church developed a strong lay leadership who brought new life, new programs, and new insight into the parish. A network of adult leaders who now extend into all areas of our parish life. A network that continues to grow.

We discovered that community is the by-product of individual believers coming together to respond to the Gospel message. You cannot make it happen. It is a gift of Jesus. And one blessed day you discover it's there among you—the gift of community, the wonder of having become a family.

On the flat roof of our church building, against the backdrop of a tall, solid, brick wall that tirelessly raises our steeple high in the air for the weary traveler to see, a small lighthouse stands, sending a light into the darkness that echoes the call of Isaiah, "Bring my sons from afar and my daughters from the ends of the earth."

Come, we are ready for you. This is the way home . . .

The Journey Home
How to be Church

Baptism—
The Sacrament of Welcome

"Is there no medicine in Gilead?
Are there no doctors there?
Why, then, have my people not been healed?"
Jeremiah 8:22

"Hello. I'm calling to find out how I go about having my baby baptized." As usual, the voice was unfamiliar and hesitant.

"You're speaking to the right person. My name's Phyllis," she said. "I'm the Pastoral Minister and I coordinate the Baptism Program. We celebrate the Sacrament of Baptism the third Sunday of every month during our 10:00 liturgy. Have you seen our baptisms before?" she asked.

"Well," came the cautious reply, "we're kind of new to the area, and just now getting settled enough to look for a church."

"You know," Phyllis said, "it's not unusual to come back to church after you have a baby. In fact, it's very normal, kind of the church cycle. You go to church with your parents when you're a child. Then, when you leave home, chances are there will be a period of time that you'll stop going. When you have a baby, you realize you want your child to have the same chance to know Jesus as you did. So you come back, and the church cycle begins for the next generation. The important thing is that you're back, and you want to make the commitment to have church be part of your child's life."

"Actually," she confessed, "we've been in the area about six years. The longer we waited to find a church, the harder it was to go back. Then, when we had the baby, we were absolutely frantic. I can't tell you how nervous I was to call. I didn't know what to expect."

3

"My friend," Phyllis said, "the door to church is always open, and the community is waiting to welcome you with open arms. What I like to do is meet with new people before the baptism to make sure they're comfortable with our liturgy, and feel this is the right church to meet their family's needs. Also, since we have the baptisms during the liturgy, I encourage families to come to a Baptism Sunday so they'll be more comfortable when they have their own. Could you and your husband meet with me this Sunday after the 10:00 Mass?" Phyllis asked.

"We'll be there," she answered, without a doubt in her voice.

"Let me write down your names," Phyllis said. "Laura and Mitch. And the baby's name is Shelly. Do you have any other children? A little girl, Sara. How old did you say she was, seven? Where about in Bellingham do you live? We have several families from our church who live near you. I think you'll find yourself quite at home here. And Laura, don't worry about bringing the baby to church on Sunday. We have many newborns. Our church is celebrated with children in mind. We like the family to be able and comfortable to come to Mass together. We have a children's Liturgy of the Word Program during the first part of the Mass that will be excellent for Sara. But we can talk more about that on Sunday. As you become part of the church family, you'll learn all the things that are available here for your own family. I'll be reading this Sunday, so you'll recognize who I am. I'll wait up front after the liturgy. Laura, I look forward to meeting with you and planning for the baptism," Phyllis said.

"I look forward to meeting with you, too," Laura replied. There was a smile in her voice.

Seven couples are coming for baptisms this month. Only one of the couples who called is active in our community. This has been the case for some years now. But the current Baptism Preparation Program is working. And through the program, most of our Baptism people are not only returning to the church, but are being "plugged" into the community.

The Baptism Preparation Program has been an excellent example of how programs will "write themselves," as we continually seek to meet the needs of an ever-changing Christian community.

This was our basic Baptism Program 10 years ago:

- The date and time for the Baptism class was listed in the church bulletin.
- Couples simply showed up on that evening. After all, they were part of the community and were quite familiar with our Baptism program.
- They were warmly greeted by the person running the class, who might do an icebreaker to introduce the people to one another.
- A filmstrip was shown on the history of the sacrament.
- Father read from Scripture and gave a theological presentation of the sacrament to the parents and godparents.
- The symbols for the sacrament were explained, including the difference between infusion and immersion baptism. We offered individual tubs for the immersions.
- At the end of the class, the couples filled out the baptism forms, listing their name, address, etc.
- The Baptism program concluded with the actual baptism, which took place the third Sunday of the month during our 10:00 liturgy.

Ten years ago this program met the needs of our community. But slowly we recognized something very frightening happening in the church. Couples were coming for a baptism because "this is what you're supposed to do when you have a baby." They were starting to be known as "the Baptism people" because they were the new people who showed up the third Sunday of the month for a baptism and never came again. The normal church cycle was being broken. What would happen in the church if parents did not come back when they had their own children?

This is when we, as church, realized that something had to change. What was in their hearts and minds as they sat silent in those chairs during the night of the Baptism class?

Since Baptism is the sacrament of welcome, it was indeed the perfect and appropriate opportunity to address these issues, to find concrete ways of drawing our "Baptism people" back into the church family. Over an eight-year period of time our current Baptism program evolved in response to this need we felt. These are the steps we gradually took over the years:

> 1) *The date and time for the Baptism class was dropped from the bulletin and replaced with: Baptism/see Father or Phyllis after Mass.*

The first step we needed was to find ways to open communication between us. Not listing the time for the class was a small but significant step in preventing people from "dropping in" the night of the class. For many varied reasons, couples who had never even been to our church were beginning to find their way to the class. And now, if someone called the rectory to find out about Baptism, they had to speak with me. I'm at the rectory everyday during the week. But if I should be out, a message was taken and I called them back.

This initial conversation between us, us representing the church, is extremely important. It is consciously warm and welcoming. The dialogue is geared to lead them into sharing where they are at concerning church. It is not unusual to speak with them for an hour. It still amazes me how great a need there is for us to listen. To assure them the door is open. It is almost as if they need our permission before they can "come home."

The conversation also provides background information and valuable insight as to what will be relevant the actual night of the class. During the conversation, plans are made to meet with their family after Mass. This is an opportunity to welcome the father and assess his feelings concerning church. It also gives the family a chance to experience the warmth of our community.

Hopefully, the conversation and the personal welcome made them feel that they are not dropping in one night to fulfill some requirements set by an impersonal institution. Rather, they are precious members of a church family who gladly stop what they are doing to welcome them in when they come knocking on the door to the House of the Lord.

We learned a lot about our Baptism people through these conversations and meetings. We discovered that the majority of the couples who came for baptism did not have a specific problem with the church. They were simply disconnected from it. Given a reason, and the support of a warm community, they could be plugged in again. Many of these couples were away from their own families, and were delighted to have this new extended church family to which they could belong.

But there were also couples who had serious issues to resolve with the church. Some had old wounds, and some even as recent as calling several churches to inquire about baptism.

We found many couples had come out of a mixture of family pressure and leftover guilt from their own religious upbringing. They had been taught that you have to have your baby baptized, so here they were. And if they answered the questions right, they could satisfy all involved.

But we did find that most couples had one essential feeling as the thread that bound us together. They all felt they had a personal relationship with Jesus. They just didn't quite understand the connection between church in their lives now, and the baptism.

And basically, these were the Baptism people. On any given Baptism night, there was a combination of all these different experiences and feelings. You could sense it in the room. Feelings safely masked beneath polite smiles. Then Father walked in, and his very presence sprinkled intimidation onto the already burdened atmosphere. On the worse nights, he'd comment to one of the couples how he hadn't seen them in church recently. His priestly training did not prepare him to relate to these Baptism people. In truth, he didn't know how it felt to be on the other side of the door, knocking to come in.

So here we all were, ready to begin the class. And many nights as the screen was being raised to show the filmstrip, it felt like a physical sign of the wall between us.

They were passing through the class, through our lives, like ships passing in the night. It was time to learn more about where they had come from. But more importantly, we needed to work together to change the direction of where they were headed.

The Baptism people had changed. We, the church, needed to find new ways to serve them.

2) Eliminate the filmstrip

As we took a closer look at the program, and the Baptism people, we arrived at this conclusion. While it made sense to watch a filmstrip with people who were part of the church family, it now seemed a loss of precious time. How could we watch a movie, so to speak, with sisters and brothers whom we hadn't seen in years?

There was too much to catch up on. They were wondering what's been happening "at home" since they've been away. Through us, they would get a feeling about what home was like these days. What have we found for our families? Is there a reason why they should come back home?

Whether we liked it or not, we faced the awesome responsibility of living the words we had often heard: "The media is the message."

Our goal now was to create a relaxed atmosphere of a family coming together. But even with two friendly conversations beforehand, most people came to the Baptism class on the defensive. Their walls were up. Simply because they'd been away for awhile, and didn't know what to expect.

We had to find a way to bring church, the institution, back to church, the family. We weren't quite sure how we would go about accomplishing this, but one thing was certain. We needed to eliminate the historical filmstrip. Instead, we began to look at the many beautiful parables in the Bible that related well to family and Baptism. Parables like the sower, the hidden treasure, or the two housebuilders. We decided to stay away from parables like the prodigal son that could evoke feelings of guilt. After Father's theological presentation of the Sacrament, we began to weave these stories into the Baptism class. And through them, we found many parallels to our own families and the church experience.

We ended every night asking that if anyone had any problem now or in the past that would keep them away from church, would they consider speaking to us about it. Baptism is a new beginning, a time to come home. We encouraged them not to let anything prevent that from happening. Church is too important a gift for our children, for our families.

Many people did speak with me after the class about specific problems and questions they had. Though we realized there were many other couples who we needed to reach, we began to see more and more Baptism people returning to church.

3) Father withdraws from the program

Father had become increasingly warmer and more friendly at the Baptism class. As he got to know these Baptism people, they often shared with him what a sensitive moment Baptism had been in their life. And it was the warm way they had been received that had made the difference of their wanting to make church a part of their lives. But no matter how friendly Father was, people were hesitant to reveal their true feelings as long as he was present.

One night an important affordable housing meeting was scheduled on the night of the Baptism class. Father missed the class. That evening two of the Baptism couples shared touching stories. Three months later, another housing meeting detained Father. Again, there was open dialogue. It was then that Father decided to withdraw from the class. He felt that the Baptism people did not need theology at that point in their lives. They needed to talk. One family sharing with another family what church meant in their lives. His prayerful decision and insight indeed made a great difference to the program.

Month after month, more and more people shared what was in their hearts concerning church. This family approach was working. They felt good about our invitation. We began to see an influx of wonderful young couples coming on Sunday, breathing new life into the community. They were excited about this extended family they had found. They each had their own unique gifts to offer the family. But we realized that if we didn't plug them into the community soon, there was a danger they would disconnect. We needed to find concrete ways to establish family ties.

4) Expanding the program

There were definite drawbacks to running the program alone. Mostly, it encouraged the new people to relate to the person running the class, rather than relating to the community. It was becoming increasingly more difficult to keep track of the returning Baptism families.

Even if the new families were noticed on Sunday, it was physically impossible for one person to greet all of them. Nothing takes the place of someone going over to you personally to make you feel like you're an important part of the family.

The solution came during one of the adult sessions of our family religious education program. Our religious education program is held monthly, beginning in September and ending in May. It includes all members of the parish from three-year-olds through adults. The adult part of our religious education program is the key to a very active laity and a strong faith community that does not see itself as complete, but searching to reach out. It also provides the community with valuable time to address issues of concern.

While children are in class, adults attend the adult session which may consist of a speaker or a film, with discussion groups following. We all study the same theme. The topic for that Sunday actually was community.

In several of the group discussions, it was brought up how many new people were joining the parish. That morning, we looked at specific ways that we, as community, could welcome them. Many questions were raised. How did they feel when they came to our liturgy? Did they feel warmly received? Were they greeted? What were their needs? How could we serve them? How could we draw these people into the family?

It was not long ago that Father shared the story of the poet Robert Burns in his homily. One day, when Robert Burns was feeling desperately lonely, he drifted into a church—and drifted out again—without having had a word or a hand of welcome. But before he left he scribbled this on the flyleaf of a hymnal:

> "As cauld a wind as ever blew;
> A caulder kirk, and in't but few;
> As cauld a minister's e'er spak':
> Ye'll all be hot ere I come back!"

Father constantly raised an awareness in all of us of the importance of welcoming the stranger in our midst, that true Christian worship has an open heart. No one wanted to find a note in our hymnals, and we were determined to find ways to welcome the stranger who walked through our doors!

Two specific ideas came out of the discussion groups. One was to initiate a newcomers' group. Seven people signed up for that committee. They would meet one Sunday a month after Mass. The C.Y.O. served coffee and donuts in the church hall every week after Mass, so the community could extend their time together in fellowship. This would be the perfect setting for the newcomers' group. People in the community would look for new people to personally extend an invitation to come to this meeting. Also, it would be announced at Mass. Hopefully, the new people themselves could express what we, as community, could do to meet their needs.

The second idea specifically addressed the Baptism people. Since most of the new people were indeed Baptism people, it was suggested that members of the community be present the night of the Baptism class simply to welcome the Baptism people into the community. Four people volunteered for this. Kim and Beth, who had recently been through the Baptism program themselves. Maureen, who was also fairly new to the community. And Mike, who had been part of the community for many years. He wanted to target the fathers who came to the class. To encourage their support of church in their own family.

They agreed to take turns coming to the class. In six months time, they decided it would be better if they all came to every class. Immediately, their presence had changed the program. It was the missing ingredient.

Each of them had something very unique to share. But, they also realized it was not easy to speak to a large group. It was a risk. They were more nervous than they had anticipated. We began to sense the strength we offered one another.

We also learned to be patient. We put the program in the Lord's hands. We knew our stories, and what we gave people in the way of sharing would evolve as we opened ourselves to the direction Jesus wanted us to take.

As the months went on, this happened. Each person's sharing became fine-tuned. The five of us were at different points in our own faith journey. We found that each Baptism couple related to a different person's experience. New stories were always being added as our own families grew in the church. But more so, as we became sensitized to the more common problems experienced by people returning to church, we added stories that addressed these concerns.

Something very powerful happened the night of the Baptism class. It was felt by everyone in the room. There was a connection made between us that went beyond the words we shared. They felt the power of the door to the House of the Lord being opened to them. Yet many still seemed to need more before they could feel like one of the family again.

5) Follow-up

For some of the Baptism families, the Baptism night was enough to reestablish their relationship with the church. The continued personal greetings on Sunday were enough to make them feel welcome. The five of us made up a small network who could greet them. Many stayed after Mass for coffee and donuts and joined the welcome committee.

But most of the families truly wanted to experience the extended family they could see we all shared. And it was this that they wanted for their own families. They wanted to break into the inner circle of friendship.

This is where the Baptism forms came in as a handy tool. We began to jot down simple observations about each family. Did the mother work days? Are they living away from their own families? Do they have older children? What was their issue with the church that kept them away? Sometimes they had a relative living with them, etc.

We used that information to link them to the community. For mothers who were home days, our playgroup was invaluable. Kim, Maureen and Beth are all leaders in the playgroup that meets every Thursday from 9:30 to 11:30 a.m. This is the best link for a family with a newborn or younger children. The playgroup publishes their own newsletter four times a year. We distribute this newsletter at the Baptism class. Through the playgroup, new mothers learn everything that we offer the community.

We have many social ministries like games night, pot luck dinners, bingo, and Holy Stitchers. The Holy Stitchers, coined by Father, are a wonderful group of women who meet every

Monday night to prepare the crafts for our annual fall family festival held in October.

We have a Summer Vacation Bible Week, a children's Liturgy of the Word Program, Jr. C.Y.O. and C.Y.O. We now have a full-time Youth Minister. She has opened a whole new realm of communication and connection for our young people. We have Serendipity Bible groups. The Serendipity is an "upper room" experience that provides a forum for Bible, support, and caring in an intimate small group setting. There is a Sunday morning Bible sharing, liturgical dance offered for the 4th graders and up, our family religious education program, the Lazarus Ministry which includes a grieving group called the Healing Hands, sacrificial giving, food pantry. And of course, our special traditional celebrations like our Christmas Eve pageant, penitential, Holy Week, sacramental programs, etc.

We have recently opened a Christian Coffeehouse, called The Lighthouse, which is held in the basement of our church hall the third Saturday of the month.

Announcements from the pulpit and the bulletin are great ways to draw attention to the time and place of these specific church happenings. But it has been our experience, that there's nothing like a one-on-one conversation to really explain things for that first time. And many people absolutely need an invitation to attend something new.

Once the new family is linked to any one of the above programs, the connection is made. They have established family ties, and from that inner group they will learn the goings-on of the church family.

Now, of course, all this works only if the Baptism people return to church. If we don't see a Baptism family for a while, a note is sent simply telling them that we miss them. It was surprising that almost every family who received a personal letter returned to church, at least for the following week. Obviously, we have to know our people to be able to recognize both who is there and who isn't. Again, the institution must be brought to the level of family.

Besides looking for these families at Mass, I have them in my drawer, so to speak. Every month I go through those yellow forms and "remember" them. Their faces come alive through the observations we have written on those sheets. The forms are indeed a physical link between us.

Oftentimes, when I go through the sheets, I'll write to the families. It could be a reminder that Summer Vacation Bible Week is coming up soon. Or simply a note asking how things are going, that we are thinking of them.

We plant a seed. We open the door. But how can we comprehend the ways Jesus meant to bring his people home?

Baptism is a magnet that constantly pulls people to Jesus and back to the church. People coming back for a baptism are like salmon trying to get back to their breeding grounds. They follow an instinct ingrained deep within, one born and bred of the spirit. If not fulfilled, there is a feeling of incompleteness. Suddenly, there is a moment that opens up in time, a moment born of that spirit, when his children come home. We, the church, must be there preparing the breeding grounds so that Jesus might be born anew in the hearts of his children.

Perhaps our greatest gift to the Baptism people is not really our years of experience with church. It is the remembering of how it felt to be on the outside looking in, before we understood the meaning of being part of a Christian community. We, the people of programs, the people of rules, must constantly remember what Jesus taught us. "The Sabbath was made for the good of man; man was not made for the Sabbath."

Catherine. Impressionable Catherine, like clay on the potter's wheel. She came to one of the Baptism classes. After the class, she and her husband stayed to talk.

"I want to be baptized along with my daughter more than anything else in the world," she confided. "I've been studying at another church for a long time." She looked ashamed. "Every week," she said, "I'd start to recite the prayers the priest gave me to learn and the same thing happened. I'd get halfway through and I couldn't remember anymore." She bit her bottom lip and her eyes were glassy. "He told me if I wasn't serious about being baptized, I should forget it. I really did study hard," she said.

They stayed till midnight, but she was silent for the rest of the conversation. She looked embarrassed as her angry young husband, while trying to defend her, also betrayed her, never noticing the difference. There was so much unspoken in those enormous, childlike eyes. Eyes looking for approval from a mother, mother church.

Father baptized Catherine on Sunday along with her daughter, whom she named Hope. Her desperate need fulfilled the law that Jesus spoke of, not the letter of the law, but the spirit of the law that was written for the good of the people.

Catherine came to church every Sunday and positively glowed. She had been born of a new womb, and felt the love and acceptance of this new mother. The church healed her as simply as Jesus did, by inviting her to take part in the banquet. We, as church, learned much through Catherine.

People come to the door of the House of the Lord like clay on the potter's wheel. Their lives are formed and shaped by the hands who receive them. And of all the moments in the church experience, perhaps Baptism is the most impressionable.

"How many chairs should we set up for tonight?" Maureen asked Kim as she walked into the room. Kim was a pretty woman. It was hard to tell her age. Her pleasant face and sparkling blue eyes gave her a girlish look. She had thick, short, brownish-black hair.

"There's seven couples coming for the class and only two of the godparents can't make it," Kim answered. "They're from out of state and won't be here till Saturday."

Maureen leaned a chair against the wall and pushed back her glasses. She was a slender woman with uncommonly soft, intelligent blue eyes. "Oh, that many," she said weakly. "I can't believe I still get so nervous doing this."

"But you always find the perfect things to share," Kim said. "And you certainly look calm."

"I couldn't even tell you what I've said when I'm done," Maureen laughed nervously. "But thanks for the vote of confidence. Do know if Mike and Beth are coming tonight?" she asked hopefully. "As far as I know," Kim answered, as she scanned the room. "Well, look's like everything's ready," she said.

The soft rose-colored room looked warm and inviting, with padded chairs set in a friendly circle on the rug. It was off the right side of the altar, and openly connected to the main church on one side. The room was formerly used as an overflow room. But tonight the smell of coffee flavored the air. Open boxes of cookies lay in waiting on the table. People began to arrive. Each month it was the same. As each small group of four arrived, they sat directly opposite one another until the circle looked like a perfectly cut pie with every other piece missing. The last people to come gradually filled in the remaining pieces. Each group was either completely silent or carefully talking to one another. No one wanted coffee.

Kim passed out the forms. Everyone concentrated on filling them out. They had just finished as Mike and Beth came in the room from the side door and Phyllis walked in through the church. She had been praying. She needed time to break down her own human defenses. She felt full of Jesus and the community. More than anything, she wanted to draw people back to the church where they could find Jesus for their family.

As she crossed the altar area, she could see the large group through the open doorway and the pretty wooden vent like window openings on either side. She willed herself to be calm. She felt the Spirit empower her as she walked into that full room. She knew what she had to offer them.

"Sorry I'm a bit late," Phyllis said, smiling warmly, taking a seat and opening her Bible all at the same time. "Let me begin by welcoming you to our Baptism class. Actually, it's not really a class. It's more of a sharing. Tonight Beth, Mike, Maureen, Kim and myself will share some of our feelings about church. We hope at some point you'll be comfortable enough to do the same. This isn't a test. There's no right or wrong answers. It's a night to be honest and to try to talk about the most important thing in our families' lives—church.

"As we go around the room, we can introduce ourselves and tell how many children we have and how long we've been in Bellingham. Also, if you're part of St. Blaise at the present time, or are you just now returning to church?

"Let me begin. My name is Phyllis. I have two children. My son Trevor is 20 and my daughter Jessie is 18. We've been at St. Blaise for about 15 years. I enjoy doing the Baptism Program. In a sense, my children are getting ready to begin their own families. Your children are just beginning their life with you. I feel like I've had a chance to see the whole picture." She smiled easily.

"We always begin the night with a reading from the Bible. Tonight, I thought we'd read the parable of the sower from Matthew's Gospel." She flipped through the pages, holding it open with her hand in place, and looked up. "The setting for this parable is quite beautiful," she said. "Jesus is near the lake where He sat down to teach. Perhaps there was a gentle breeze coming in off the water. And there were so many people who wanted to hear this man from Galilee, that Jesus got into a boat. He went a little way from shore and slowly He began to tell them the parable of the sower."

> *Once there was a man who went out to sow grain. As he scattered the seed in the field, some of it fell along the path, and the birds came and ate it up. Some of it fell on rocky ground, where there was little soil. The seeds soon sprouted, because the soil wasn't deep. But when the sun came up, it burned the young plants; and because the roots had not grown deep enough, the plants soon dried up.*

She read slowly, with great feeling, looking deeply into each face as she read. She felt the connection between them was already beginning. She continued to read the passage.

> *Some of the seed fell among thorn bushes, which grew up and choked the plants. But some seeds fell in good soil, and the plants bore grain: some had one hundred grains, others sixty, and others thirty. And Jesus concluded, 'Listen, then, if you have ears!'*

She closed the Bible but still held the place with her hand. "When Jesus finished this parable," she said, "the disciples asked Him to explain what it meant. I wish they would have asked Him to explain all of them," she said smiling. "But this is the explanation He gave to them."

She opened the Bible and began to read again.

> *Listen, then, and learn what the parable of the sower means. Those who hear the message about the Kingdom but do not understand it are like the seeds that fell along the path. The evil one comes and snatches away what was sown in them. The seeds that fell on rocky ground stand for those who receive the message gladly as soon as they hear it. But it does not sink deep into them, and they don't last long. So when trouble or persecution comes because of the message, they give up at once.*

Her voice began to rise as it sought to transmit the power of the words.

> *And the seeds that fell among thorn bushes stand for those who hear the message; but the worries about this life and the love for riches choke the message, and they don't bear fruit. And the seeds sown in the good soil,*

her voice seemed to caress the words,

> *'and the seeds sown in the good soil,'* she repeated, *'stand for those who hear the message and understand it: they bear fruit, some as much as one hundred, others sixty, and others thirty.'*

She gently closed the Bible, stood up and glanced intensely around the room. You could hear a pin drop. "Baptism," she began, "is the sacrament of the seed and the fruit."

"When we were children growing up in our own families, our life was basically carefree. Oh, you might have had some assigned chores, about which you complained bitterly," she smiled, her blue eyes filled with the memory, "but life centered around you. This was a time in your life where your needs were met. Things were kind of simple, too. There was a basic set of house rules to follow, rules you were not allowed to question. And who doesn't remember the "Why, because I said so!" routine? And though as children we couldn't always see the wisdom behind the rules, we definitely saw the wisdom in keeping them.

"Our world was one of yes and no. If your parents said no, it was definitely because they didn't love you. When you got older, if they said no, it translated to they didn't trust you. Why was it, I wonder, that as much as your parents loved you and cared for you, and as often as you saw and hated to admit they were right time and time again, it seemed like they were on one side and you were on the other. Your relationship was a constant tug-of-war. You truly believed in your heart that they didn't understand what you were going through.

"Then there were THOSE THINGS they did that made you so angry. I was the second child, and when my older sister bossed me around or we had a fight, I wanted my mother to be the judge. And nothing, absolutely nothing in the whole world made me angrier than when my mother would tell me that I had to work it out for myself. Easy for her to say when my sister was bigger and could push me around. Why couldn't she understand that she should just punish my sister like she deserved? The issues involved were clear cut to me.

"There was only one thing that I hated more, and that was when my mother gave me the silent treatment. And I swore, then, that I would never, never do these things to my own children. Sound familiar?" she laughed.

"Now the parents with older children know exactly what I mean. It doesn't take long before you find yourself sounding and acting exactly like your own parents. And what a shock it is the first time it happens. Without knowing how or exactly when it happened, you somehow crossed over to that other side, the parent's side, and now you find yourself looking into a mirror of your own childhood. You see yourself in the reflection of those defiant little faces, now your children, telling you how you just don't understand anything.

"Slowly, all the wisdom behind those house rules are revealed until you see how much love was behind each one. A love you couldn't understand with a child's vision of things. And how it just kills you to look back and see how much your parents did for you. How you complained over clearing the table and cleaning your own room. Through your own children you begin to understand how well your own parents really knew you. How deeply they loved you to insist on being the parent when they knew you sometimes hated them for it. How they would have taken your pain if they could. How they often did. How they wished you didn't have to ever be hurt.

"Once, I remember telling my mother how I wished I could somehow repay her for all she's done for me. You know what my mother told me? She said that's how the family works. She said her mother did those same things for her and she didn't see it until she had her own children. Now she did these things for me, and it's my turn to do the same for my own children. One day my children will see things from the other side.

"That's a parent's repayment, when their children come back home as friends. The tug-of-war is over. There's no more need of house rules. The parent-child relationship slips into a beautiful time of friendship. Before I left that morning and many times since, I tell my mother how much I love her. I ask for her advice, linger in her presence, visit more often. And most of all, treasure this golden time we have together. We find ourselves bearing fruit, as much as one hundred, because the soil was so rich."

"Now," she continued, "we also grow up in another house, the House of the Lord. And much the same thing occurs. We have a parent-child relationship with Jesus and are given a set of house rules to follow. Remember being little and thinking that Jesus was waiting for us to do something wrong, not even to do it, just to think about doing it. And He was going to punish us, to get us one day?

"Prayer was quite simple, too. We asked Jesus for what we wanted. If we didn't get it, then Jesus didn't answer our prayers. But here's the tricky part in our relationship with Jesus." She stopped thoughtfully and made eye contact with each one in the room. "Some people never come back home after they grow up. They never return to church, to the Lord's House. These people, and it doesn't matter how old they get," she said waving her hand in the air, "will always see Jesus from a child's point of view. Jesus will remain locked in a parent child relationship.

"So many people you hear today say they've outgrown the need for church. There's nothing there for them anymore, they insist. Do you believe," she asked directly, "do you believe that Jesus depends on us to fulfill His plan? That He might need us?

"For 18 years we are a seed in the church family." She put her hands together to form a seed. "We are concerned with us.

Praying for our needs, for our desires, asking our questions. But there is a purpose in preparing the fertile ground all those years. That purpose is for every child to come back home to the church family and to begin to give back to the family. Only when you come back can you see things from that magic other side," she grinned.

"Now you see the reason behind the rules. Reasons a 7-year-old can't comprehend. And I promise you, all those things, the words of Jesus in the Gospel, will be revealed to you in time, as you see Scripture with adult eyes. Now the rod you saw as a child will turn into a staff as Jesus slips from parent to friend.

"And one day, you will be sitting at His table and you will find yourself saying: 'I wish I could somehow repay you for all you've done for me.' Jesus is waiting for this moment. For the second stage of your relationship with Him. When you want to linger, to visit often. When you ask for His advice, seek His wisdom. He will show you what to do. The rest of your life will be spent returning to Him. Some as much as one hundred, others sixty and others thirty, depending on the richness of the soil.

"For many of you tonight, this is your first visit home in many years. But that's okay. In a way it's even good. Now your faith is your own, not your parents'. You have come back freely. And you want your children to have the same chance to know Jesus as you were given. Two things will happen when you come back. For 18 years, you will have the chance to prepare the soil for your own children. What kind of soil will you prepare?" she said and paused.

"At the same time, you will have the chance to return your own gifts to the Lord. For truly, Baptism is the sacrament of the seed and the fruit."

Again she paused and seemed to try to reach into each one's heart. After a brief silence Kim said, "I guess I'll go next."

"Hi, I'm Kim," she began. "I have three children. My son Matthew is 10. My daughter Ryan is eight and my other daughter Kerrin is four. My husband is Michael. We have had all of our children baptized here at St. Blaise. But it has only been the last four years that I have been coming to Mass regularly.

"After Matthew was born, we felt truly blessed. We thought that the birth of our baby was such a miracle, and that our son was a gift from God. We didn't know it when we picked his name, but Matthew means Gift of God. We started to come back to church but we never got into the habit of planning to get up on Sunday morning. Soon Sundays slipped back to being just another day of the week.

"When Ryan was born, the same thing happened. This time, knowing that we weren't regularly attending Mass, it was difficult to come back to ask for another baptism. But we did, and she was baptized. Trying to fit Sunday morning Mass into the schedule with two small kids was hard. Again, we found the only times we came to Mass were Christmas and Easter, always feeling hypocritical and out of place, I might add. After Kerrin was born, with a lot of reluctance and guilt, because we still weren't coming, we called about having her baptized. We always knew that church had a place in our family. We knew sooner or later we'd catch hold of that thread again. That our kids would make their First Communion and Confirmation was never a question in our minds."

She grabbed the seat of her chair before going on.

"But this time something changed. I wasn't sure if it was the new baby or the fact that Matthew was entering first grade and close to making his First Communion. Maybe it was a combination of the two that caused me to realize I needed church in my life. And it started out just that way—church in my life.

"I started to come to Mass on Saturday night, alone. It was very quiet and peaceful. I would leave with a sense of well-being and my patience was renewed. But something different happened this time. It surprised me how often during the Gospel, and especially the homily, the words seemed to jump right out as if they had been spoken just for me. I realized that I was hearing the words for the first time as an adult, not as a child or a rebellious teenager. Jesus was talking to me where I was at in my life. And suddenly, without quite knowing why, it became very important for me to start taking my children to Him. Sometimes Kerrin would stay home with Michael. She was real fidgety and it was easier to leave her home with him since he wasn't coming with us. For a while it really bothered me that he stayed home while the rest of us went. But I had to work this out for myself and I hoped he would too. We had always wanted church to be a part of our life. But things that had happened at other churches were still keeping us away.

"At one point, years ago, Michael wanted to go to Sunday morning Bible at our church, but I said NO WAY! Funny how we let each other's opinions stop ourselves from doing what we instinctively would have liked to do," she said reflectively. "Now I was kicking myself for putting a halt to that urge. Every week I'd ask if he would be coming with us. He'd say no, or maybe but then wouldn't get up in time. Then Matthew started to ask if Dad was coming. One Sunday I stopped answering for Michael. I told Matthew I couldn't answer for Daddy and he would have to ask him himself. Baseball season was over and Michael didn't have a good enough reason to tell his son why he was staying home, so Michael started coming with us.

"The first Sunday he came, the kids fought to sit near him and held onto his arm the entire Mass. They even refused to leave with the other children when it was time to go downstairs for the children's Liturgy of the Word, which they absolutely love. That's their special time during the Mass. It was almost as if they were afraid if they let go, Michael would be gone when they got back. One Sunday shortly after that, during the Our Father, we all hold hands during the Our Father, I held Michael's hand just a little tighter than usual. I prayed that he would find some trace of what I found at Mass each week. He's been coming with us ever since.

"And with all that's happened to our family at church, I wish I could sit here and tell you it's now easy to come every week. But, it's like everything else in your life, you have to constantly work at it."

She took a deep breath and shifted the position in her chair. Her thick brown hair bounced about her face. A blush crept up her cheeks, making her blue eyes even bluer. The people enjoyed the casual way she shared and quietly waited for her to continue.

"One night before a Baptism meeting," she said, "I was trying to think of something to share with the group. I usually try to have some thought to take with me for fear of not having anything to say," she confided.

"An idea came to me to tell the story of how earlier that day I had decided to make a basket, a rather simple round basket. Earlier in the year a friend had shown me how to weave an Easter basket with a fancy handle and decorative curls on the side.

Quite detailed for a first try. It came out beautiful. I thought this simple basket would be no problem.

"Since I was so sure of my ability, I set right to work and started weaving away, not really paying attention to what I was doing." Her hands moved like she was weaving. "I even made a few phone calls while I was working on it. When I got to the last step I anchored the last reed. I confidently gave the rim a final tug to check its sturdiness and the whole rim came off!" Her eyes widened with expression. "I couldn't believe it. All that work." She paused with her hands in the air. "If I had been paying closer attention to what I was doing, I wouldn't have cut off the reeds that anchor the rim. I would have had the basket I intended to make." She looked serious.

"What happened that day made me think that teaching the children about Jesus is a lot like weaving a basket," she said. "If you don't pay close attention to the weave, you won't be happy with what you have in the end. When your children leave home and someone gives a real tug on them, the whole rim will come off, so to speak. And the scary part is, that's one basket you can't make over again."

Her lips were set in a mother's teaching look as she glanced around the room. Then she looked down to her lap to disconnect the eye contact.

"Kim, I absolutely love that basket story," Phyllis said. "Nothing could be truer. You've all heard the expression, 'Life begins at 40,'" she continued. "Well, that always puzzled me until I turned 40 last year. I'm beginning to figure out what it means. By the time you're 40 the kids are gone, and the honeymoon begins again," she said laughing.

"Seriously, though, the mystery of life is that every stage, from the time your children are born to the time they leave home, is beautiful. I used to insist that I'd never want my children to be on their own. But you find yourself ready for that too. It's the natural order of family life. At this stage in my own life, I realize my time is my own again. I can go back to school if I want, change my career, even begin piano lessons again. I can do anything." She slowed her speech. "I can do anything," she repeated, "except one thing." She leaned over on her chair and pointed her index finger in the air. "I can't say to my children, 'Come back, I forgot to tell you about Jesus.'"

"Last September when Trevor left for college, it hit me that what we taught him was basically finished. And for good or for bad, he was walking out our door taking it with him. We couldn't change it. We couldn't start over. Like Kim said, the basket was made. I don't know if Trevor will keep Jesus in His life forever. I hope he will. But I know that I've done my part. What they do after that is their responsibility.

"Tonight is a night of decision." Again she looked deeply into each one's face. "No one can or should tell you that you have to go to church. Each person has to decide that for themselves. And even if there was a rule that said you had to come to church for one whole year before you were allowed to have your baby baptized, it wouldn't matter. You can sit in a bench on Sunday your whole life and never hear the Word. You have to want Jesus. You have to want to be open to Him. No one can make that happen for you," she said and looked directly over to Beth.

"I guess it's my turn," Beth said in her good-natured way. Beth had a rosy apple complexion with chestnut-colored eyes. Her shoulder-length reddish brown hair was tied back simply with a ribbon. She wore a bib jumper. One would never guess she was a born-and-raised city girl.

"Hi, my name is Beth," she said. "I have three kids, Emily who just turned four, Jeffrey who will be three in August, and Daniel who just turned one year. I have been coming here to St. Blaise for just about four years. I guess I'll start by telling you how I got here."

She slid down in the chair as she spoke. "When I was pregnant with my daughter, I figured I better find a church so I could get her baptized. My husband Tom and I had been away from church for years. I was pretty much on my own looking for a church. But Tom had said he would go if I found a reasonable place.

"Well, let me tell you I shopped and shopped. We were an hour away at the time, and I went to all the churches in the surrounding area. Finally, after going to about 15 different churches, I settled on one. What a mistake! All I had to do to join was fill out a little white card with my name and drop it in the collection basket. No one ever talked to me until a man showed up at our house looking for donations toward turning the school building into a parish center, and donations started at $500.00

Can you believe it? We had no money, so the man left and no one ever bothered us again. Needless to say, Tom was not impressed with my choice of church.

"In the meantime, my sister Barbara had moved here to Bellingham and suggested we check out the church they had joined. I can't remember, but I think the first service we attended was Christmas Eve. It was unbelievable. Dancing, singing, kids everywhere, not to mention a real live donkey. And a sign of peace that took 15 minutes. Both Tom and I loved it. So I convinced my sister to talk with Phyllis about having our baby baptized there. I was afraid that we would be turned down, so I certainly didn't want to ask. So Barbara did. Of course, we were welcomed with open arms; no red tape, no questions, and no note from our church. I can't tell you what a relief this was!

"So we came to Baptism class with Emily in tow. And I must tell you I don't envy where you are at right now. This is an awesome decision, to commit your child to a Catholic upbringing. Getting to church every Sunday is no easy task. When we were leaving the class, I remember telling Phyllis I didn't know if we would make it here every week, you know, a 45-minute drive. She calmly looked at me and said, 'Well, people commute an hour or more to their jobs, why not church?'"

"I said that?" Phyllis quipped, with a friendly laugh.

"What could I say?" Beth continued with her effervescent smile. "I was so overwhelmed with the sense of commitment that I was entering into. My husband, on the other hand, couldn't understand my problem. All he said was, 'This is what you've been looking for, right?'"

"And it was right. So we came to Mass almost every week. In the meantime we moved to Taunton. How great, now church was only 20 minutes away. We actually live in Bellingham, now, about 5 minutes away from church. I honestly believe that through some very difficult times Jesus led us closer and closer to this community. I look back and think of how he really had to knock us over the head to get us here. And hindsight is a wonderful gift, because we would not have survived the birth of our third child if it hadn't been for this community.

"Wait," she said, holding her hands out and looking quite like an excited child with her fresh-scrubbed, wholesome face. "Before Daniel was born I was really nervous. Never mind what was going on financially, but how would I ever handle three kids under three? I was really stressed out about everything. But let me tell you, the first two weeks I was home with Daniel I never cooked. I mean people got together and planned our dinners. We have never, or will never eat so well again." She beamed. "One woman even offered to do laundry for me. It was and is an unbelievable phenomena to have something so special happen. People I hardly knew sent us unbelievable meals, including wine and dessert. So you might be feeling that you're making a huge commitment, but there is an entire group here who want to see you succeed in this. And will support and love you throughout.

"I think the greatest thing about church that has changed since I was a child is this new sense of community. When I was growing up, you went to church, and it was you and God. Maybe that's part of the reason I felt I didn't need church in my life to experience Him.

"Now, it's more the feeling that we are the family of God. You and me." She extended her hand to all of them. "We cannot be church unless we care for one another. Our table must be open to everyone." "Everyone," she emphasized. "Jesus healed people simply by letting them know they were welcome around the table. We must do the same. We are welcoming you into our church family. No conditions. And we hope to know you as part of our family. Well, I guess that's all I have to say."

Mike was next. He was a handsome man with dark hair and boyish brown eyes. He had a dimple in his chin. He was built like an athlete.

"Hello," he began. "I'm Mike. I am married with three children, all boys, with the oldest being 14 and the youngest 9." He folded his arms across his chest as he continued to speak. "I have been a member of the St. Blaise community for about 10 years," he said. "Like many other people you talk with, or have listened to this evening, my wife and I were going through tough times on making the decision of what church to attend. And we were having personal struggles if we were going to go to church at all. I think what really helped us come to a final decision was that we thought it was important for us, as parents, to teach our children about God and Jesus, and how it applies to everyday life.

"My wife and I consider ourselves very fortunate that we are part of a strong community. The story I can tell to best show

how this community has affected my children is the one about a situation that occurred at Parent's Night at my son's school. My middle-aged son Matthew was 10 years old at the time. My wife and I were walking around in the classroom when his teacher challenged each parent to find their child's self-portrait. The pictures were spread around the desk and the countertops in the classroom. I must admit that they all looked the same, bearing strong resemblances to the cartoon characters that they all watched." He broke into a chuckle and shook his head. "My wife and I had thought we had it narrowed down to a couple of portraits, but couldn't decide, so we kept looking, when we came upon a picture that was unmistakably our son's. We told his teacher we had found our son's portrait. He smiled and told us to keep looking to make sure. My wife told him that we both knew this was his and we didn't have to look any further. His teacher looked on the back and told us we were correct, and questioned us on how we were so sure.

"The one item that made his portrait different from every other one in the room was the small wooden cross worn around his neck that is so common to the community members here at St. Blaise." He reached into his soft white, gray and red knit jersey for the wooden cross that hung around his own neck. As he pulled out the black nylon cord, his fingers lovingly sought the smooth cross. He tenderly held it between his thumb and index finger to give everyone a better look. Eyes drifted across the room resting on each of the plain brown carved wooden crosses that Beth, Kim, Maureen and Phyllis also wore. "We felt elated," Mike said, "that he was so comfortable with Jesus that he could portray it in this way. It really made our day."

"That was a very important moment in our life as parents. The point I would like to stress here is to give to your children the best life possible. To go to church regularly, and bring your family with you. You have brought them into this world, now it's up to you to carry on with the tradition of teaching them what is right and wrong. Don't wait till they are 18 to start to teach them." "Then," he concluded, "it will be too late, your work will already be done."

"Thanks, Mike," Phyllis said. "At this time, I like to speak in particular to the fathers who are here this evening."

Suddenly it appeared as if something very interesting was happening on the rug as all eyes were drawn to it, carefully avoiding the possibility of eye contact. "Again," Phyllis said, "let me assure you that I'm not here to make you feel guilty, although my two children tell me I'm quite good at it." This time the tension eased quickly.

"It would be easy if children learned by us telling them what to do," she said. "But we all know that is not the case. Children learn by how we live. And if you, as fathers, tell your child that church is important, that you want them to go, and then you don't go to church yourself, then what you're really saying is that you don't think it's important at all.

"Try this some time. Take a piece of paper and have everyone in the family list the 10 things they think are the most important in each other's life. How many families today would list church in the top five, or even the top ten?

"Just for fun, I asked my niece, who is only six, to tell me what she thought her father loved to do best. In two seconds she said hockey. Now, my brother has been known to play hockey at midnight after working hard all day because that's the only time he and his friends can rent the ice. Yet, this same brother will tell me that the 10:00 Sunday liturgy is too inconvenient." Everyone laughed and one of the mothers inconspicuously touched her husband's arm. "The bottom line is," Phyllis continued, making direct eye contact with each father, "whatever is a priority in our life we will find a way to make time for.

"If you have a son, you will be the role model. This is the case in two-parent families. You cannot escape this. Your son will be watching you to see if a man needs God in his life, if a man needs church in his life. Or is it just for mothers and daughters? And if you don't go to Mass, the trouble will most likely begin when your son reaches 13, just the time you'll want him to go.

"Now, if you have a girl, don't think you get off the hook that easily. When I was growing up, we always went to church as a family. We were six children. My mother was the real serious one about church. You know, still saying her rosary ten minutes after the Mass was over. But church was a family experience and a warm memory of family in my life. So, it was natural for me to see church in this light. When I had my own family, I just assumed my husband would come with me. I wonder if this would have been the case if my father hadn't been part of church in my own childhood.

"Again, I'm not trying to tell you what to do, but I don't want you to leave here tonight with any doubt that you are a role model for your children, whether you choose to be or not. Only you can decide if you consider it your responsibility as a father to bring your children to God.

"I often wonder, when we meet Jesus in person, and we certainly will one day, what excuse will be good enough to give why we didn't have time to bring our children to Him." She let the words hang in the air for several moments.

"Oh, it's my turn," Maureen said softly. "It's always so hard to know where to begin." She drew one leg up in the chair and held it. "I guess I'll start by introducing myself. My name is Maureen. I started coming to St. Blaise when my daughter was a year and a half old. Emily is now five and a half and my son Tyler is three and a half. I've been working in the Baptism program for about two years. You'd never know it by the way I still get so nervous," she said rubbing her hands together. "But I'll try to do justice to the feelings here." She pushed her glasses back against her meek blue eyes.

"Neither of my children were baptized here," she began. "I had grown away from church in college, and had made only half-hearted attempts to return during the years between graduation and the birth of my first child. When it came time to have Emily baptized, my parents made arrangements for the ceremony to take place in the parish in which I was raised. Since I had no ties to any of the churches in this area, I was content with this plan.

"The quiet and very lovely christening was held in the convent chapel and was performed by a priest who has been a friend of the family for many years. The only thing I had to do in preparation for this event was get permission from the pastor of my current parish to have Emily baptized elsewhere.

"So, one day, I gathered up my courage to call the rectory, expecting full well to suffer the guilt trip of a lifetime. The phone conversation was even worse than I had anticipated. How could I expect a priest to okay my daughter's baptism when he couldn't be sure that I would raise her to be a good Catholic? After all, he didn't know me, did he? Had he seen me at Mass lately?

"The palms of my hands were sweaty, my stomach ached, and my heart was thumping wildly. He wanted me to go face-to-face with him the next morning! Our meeting the following day was quick, brief and ended with the warning, 'I'll be seeing you at Mass from now on, won't I!' We did go back a couple times, but we felt that children there were expected to be seen and not heard, so we soon stopped attending.

"When my son Tyler was born, I had been attending St. Blaise for about four months. As the time for his baptism drew near, I was, once again, faced with the horrid task of asking permission to have my child christened at my parent's parish. I still felt new to the church and, honestly, I could not believe that any Catholic church would be so very different from the last one I had attended that they would accept me after having been away for so long.

"Fearful of going through the same scene again, I couldn't make myself approach the pastor at St. Blaise. I arrived at my parent's home, a three hour car ride from here, without the permission, willing to take my chance. Fortunately, the Sisters who were allowing us to use their chapel covered for me. They made no mention of the missing permission until after the ceremony, since, they reasoned, no one could 'un-baptize' my baby.

"As beautiful as my children's baptisms were, I am still a little sorry that we didn't have our children baptized here. I feel like we skipped an important step in the development of our relationship with this community. Instead of the quiet, private services we had, we could have been a part of the joyful, very informal celebration here. A few years ago, though, that idea probably would have been a bit frightening. But as we've gotten to know this congregation, our ideas on religion have changed, along with other basic questions we struggled with when we had our own children. Things like, should we force our children to go to church? I certainly remember telling my own parents that when I had children of my own I would never make them go to church if they didn't want to. I know some of you have older children and might be facing this question of whether or not to force your children to go to church every Sunday and be like our own parents were. Force them!" she said heartily.

"Believe me, no matter how much children enjoy church, and they will truly like it here, few children are going to get up on Sunday morning and say, 'Please, Mom and Dad, take me to church.' " At this, they all laughed. "Although it's been known to happen," she continued, "that's the exception."

"The truth is, children of the 90s are given too many choices. By the time they choose the outfit they want to wear for the day, their toys, their breakfast, etc., the parents are completely stressed out before their work day even begins. We are a product of overreacting to our being told, 'You'll do as I say.' Yet, a child needs simple rules to feel secure. They need to feel not only that you're in charge, but that you are sure of what you want. As soon as your child realizes you are going to church every week, no matter what, they will accept it as they do going to school. If, on the other hand, they know their behavior, or should I say lack of behavior, will affect your decision, you can count on a sure fight every Sunday.

"It's safe to say that the routine in every house is pretty much the same. You fight with the children five days a week to get them up and ready for school. On Saturday the kids are up bright and early at six o'clock in the morning, watching cartoons and coming in during the commercials asking for their cereal. Then, on Sunday, it's like a sleeping spell has been cast over the entire house. No amount of noise would wake the children. And after a restless night, suddenly no matter which way you turn you can't get comfortable. You lay there faced with the monumental decision, should I disturb this one chance I have to rest all week or should I wake the family?

"And there is no one to answer to if you decide not to go. At least when you miss work, you have to face the boss the next day. But when it comes to church you have only yourself for motivation. Only you and Jesus to work this out. And if Jesus becomes a distant memory, it will be easier and easier to stay away from church entirely. Get into the routine of coming to church now. The only way that kids are going to be comfortable in God's house is if they visit it often.

"When I look at the teenagers in this parish, I am amazed by their involvement and commitment to church. They want to be a part of this community and make a difference. That's what I want for my kids. My greatest wish for them is that they will find the love and peace and comfort that comes from a strong relationship with Jesus and the church.

"If they can rely on a spiritual strength to get them through all the stages of their lives, I know that they will always be happy people. I hope that all made sense," she finished in her humble way.

Slowly, as Phyllis, Kim, Beth, Mike and Maureen had shared their down-to-earth, honest feelings about church, the walls had come down. The mood had been created. People were relaxed. The institution had been brought to the level of family. Their openness and, yes, their own struggle to regain church in their lives now gave the Baptism people permission to share their own struggle and questions concerning church.

"Why don't we stop for a moment," Phyllis suggested, "and have some coffee and pastries before we continue. Feel free to help yourself." Everyone was quick to get up and moved around the tables reaching for cookies, pouring coffee and talking openly to each other. After a few minutes, when they had slowly drifted back to their seats, Phyllis spoke again.

"What we'd like to do now is go around the room and you can introduce yourself. If you'd like, you can share something about church, but you don't have to," she said. "Why don't we start with you, Jim, since you're an old pro at this," Phyllis said.

Jim smiled pleasantly. His long legs were crossed at the ankles, his worn construction boots comfortably resting together. He was still dressed in work clothes. An empty hammer holster hung from his belt. "My name's Jim," he said, "and this is my wife Katie." He pointed to the tall, dark-haired woman by his side. "The godparents are my brother Bill and his wife Anne." They both nodded.

"I have a 10-year-old daughter, Mary, from a previous marriage, a 4-year-old girl, Cindy, and a month-old baby, Bethany. We've been coming here for quite some time now. I purposely mentioned my previous marriage because that's how we got involved here. Since the divorce we didn't feel so welcome at church. But when we got custody of Mary, we were worried about her CCD. So we came to talk to Father about enrolling Mary in the program. We really weren't thinking of coming ourselves.

"Then Father told us they have a family education program and said how much we'd love it. I remember looking at my wife and not knowing what to say. She looked at me as if to say, we can't very well lie to a priest. So I told him we were divorced, that this was the second marriage for both of us.

"We expected a quick cold shoulder, but he laughed and said. 'It's about time priests get out of the marriage business, don't you think?' Then he placed his arm on my shoulder in a friendly manner and asked if we were serious about church. For some reason what he told us that day really stuck.

"He told us that Mary's not going to learn about Jesus from a book. She's going to learn about Jesus at home from the way we live our lives. 'You and your wife will be her real teachers,' he said. 'Parents can't send their kids off to learn religion. Church will only be important to her if it is to us.' That was really new to me," he said shaking his head.

"Then he asked us again if we were serious about church. We're serious, I told him, and boy, I meant it. So we enrolled in the parish and the religious education program. To tell you the truth, I really didn't think I needed it. But, at that point, I certainly wasn't going to rock the boat. Here I was an altar boy, having gone to Catholic school all my life. I thought I knew everything there was to know about church. And either the church has changed an awful lot, or I have, but I know I get more out of the education program than my kids do.

"I mean, let's face it," he said, "when we were little everything was a sin. In all honesty, half of me wanted Mary to go to CCD, but the other half didn't want her to grow up with the kind of Catholic guilt I had heaped on me. I wanted my kids to have church in their lives, yet I had a lot of resentment for the way I felt about church and some of the things I was taught."

He shook his head again. "It was all very confusing. But I'm glad I'm back and I can't believe how different it is now. Take it from me. Just come, and you'll be happy you did." He leaned back, almost surprised at all he had to say, and let out a sigh of relief.

"It really helps to hear that," the woman seated near Jim said earnestly. "I don't want Sara, my daughter, to grow up feeling guilty about everything, the way I did. By the way, I'm Laura. This is my husband Mitch and the godparents Mark and Meghan. Besides Sara, we have a little baby named Shelly. I'm hesitant to even say how long I've been away from church. Let's just say it's been awhile. What bothers me most, I guess, is how I felt calling for the Baptism. It was just like Maureen described. I had to ask myself,' 'Do I want to go back to a place that makes me feel like this?' And of even more concern, 'Is this what I want for my children?' When I finally got my courage up to call the rectory, I couldn't believe how friendly and easy the conversation had gone. It was only afterwards when I hung up, that I asked myself, 'Why didn't I expect that kind of warm response from the church?' So, I'm sitting here with very mixed feelings."

"There's one thing you have to remember," Phyllis said. "And we talked about it a lot tonight. Your memories of church are from your childhood, so your experience is coming from that point of view. You also have to take into consideration that your children are coming to a very different church experience. They're not being plugged into the world as we knew it, so why should we expect them to be plugged into the church as we knew it? The Word of God never changes, but the church has to be a reflection of the time, or it isn't relevant to people's lives.

"The church was different for our parents, it was different for us, and it will be different for our children. Just one example. The children today begin their confession by saying one good thing about themselves. How's that for change? The focus is not on sin as much as on our entire relationship with God. In 20 years we've learned a lot about parenting, psychology, new Bible scholarship, etc. This new learning is not lost on the church. You can't stand in the 90s with all the knowledge we have and look back and judge the church of the 60s and 70s. We can't take the church out of its time. There is a whole new church experience waiting for both you and your children. But you have to come back to find this out for yourself," Phyllis concluded. Laura seemed content with this explanation.

"Now, you're Peter and Madeline, right?" Phyllis asked. "If I remember correctly, you're not from Bellingham. I forgot why you decided to come here for your baptism," she prompted. She distinctly recalled how the sound in his voice the day he called the rectory had triggered off an alarm in her. Also, it was unusual to have a father call for baptism.

"I told you on the phone that I called because of friends we knew who came here. And that we wanted to come here as well," he said. "That was half true, and believe me, I had no intention of going into this tonight. In fact, I planned to have this baptism and that was going to be it for me and church."

He moved his hands in a calling-it-quits gesture. His jaw tightened as he continued to speak. "I called three different churches to inquire about a baptism and was treated so rudely I would have forgotten the whole thing if it didn't mean so much to my wife Madeline." She looked the picture of a "steel magnolia," sitting by his side, having this delicate strength about her. "A business could never get away with treating people the way some churches do, or they wouldn't stay in business for long," he said. His neat blue trousers and pin-striped shirt seemed a witness to his knowledge in this area. "This is my third child," he said. "Do I have a right to have her baptized without an inquisition from the church? Granted, we haven't been to church too often since our second baby was born, but this attitude will never get us back." He sat back in his chair, folded his arms over his chest, and looked like he hoped there would be an answer that his logical mind could accept.

"Let me first say one thing in defense of church," Phyllis began, "and this is in no way to excuse rudeness. Sacraments are only visible signs. Like Father Connolly often says, the Sacrament of Marriage doesn't make two people love one another. It celebrates the love that already exists. In the same way, we celebrate your faith and commitment and welcome your family into community through the Sacrament of Baptism.

"Baptism doesn't make your child a child of God. Every child in the whole world is a child of God. Baptism is a celebration of your promise to bring your child into the community to know Him. Many times when a person calls for a baptism, or First Communion, or a wedding, they haven't been to church in years. They want to drop in, so to speak, have the baptism or wedding, whatever the sacrament, and that's it, no commitment on their part. And we'll see them at the next appropriate sacrament. In the church circle it's called the 777 Club.

"The problem is finding a delicate, warm way to handle an extremely touchy situation. No child should be refused baptism, you're right. But at the same time, what is the meaning of baptism if the parents never come back to church? People have to make the final decision about church and Jesus in their life, but the church cannot allow the sacraments to become empty shells.

"Church has a responsibility to make people aware that there is a commitment involved in receiving a sacrament. In the early church people studied for a full year before they were received into the full worshipping community. Today, people do not want any demands put on them. And the less people are involved in church life, the more they resent anything that sounds remotely like a demand. So, how do we, as church, find a balance? This is our side, the problem we struggle with.

"I am not in any way trying to excuse what happened and how you were treated," Phyllis continued. "But people are human, and things like this will occur and continue to occur as long as church is run by humans." She thought a moment before continuing.

"When my son was seven, he wanted to play baseball in the worst way. So we signed him up for one of those pre-little league teams. The coach looked like an ex-Marine. There were two teams practicing and his son was one of the players on the same team my son was on.

"My son and four other little seven-year-olds sat shyly on the bench watching this coach totally humiliate his son with every play. He screamed at all of them like the team was in the play-offs for the World Series. Suddenly he stormed over to these five little boys, put his hands on his hips and yelled, 'Who wants to go up next?' The boys looked at one another, scared half to death. Before anyone had a chance to say anything, he turned in a rage and shouted. 'Well, if none of you want to play, then stay on the bench!'

"The boys were shaking and I don't ever remember being so angry at anyone in my life. Or feeling so helpless, knowing there was no reasoning with this man. But what I do remember is that I never considered giving up the idea of my son playing baseball because of this one coach.

"Yet, when it comes to church, you hear people say, 'I don't go anymore because one time a priest told my uncle's cousin's sister's best friend. . . .' " She dropped her hand. "You know what I'm saying," she said. "The same thing happens in every other aspect of our lives. But we are conditioned to handle it differently.

"Church must become so important in our lives that no one will make us give it up. Church must be something we actually feel our family needs to survive. As essential as our jobs, as our food, our clothing, our shelter. Important enough to say, 'I won't give up until I find the right church for my family.' The bottom line is, whatever is a priority in our lives, we will find a way to do it." As she finished, Peter's wife put her arm around him.

"My name's Meghan," a pretty, middle-aged woman said. "I'm the godmother for Laura and Mitch's baby. I come from the Midwest and do feel that church is essential for our family. But I find myself in quite a dilemma with my young daughter." She looked at the group. "I hope you don't mind my asking this at the baptism, but it's something that's really been bothering me.

"My daughter loves church and wants to be an altar girl in the worst way. Some of her friends are altar girls in the next parish over and she can't understand why she can't be. The pastor of our church flatly refuses to have girls as servers and my daughter is crushed. He won't even discuss the issue. I've been told that there is no official ruling on this matter, and each priest makes his own decision.

"I guess I was brought up to go to church where we belonged, no matter what," she said. "Are you suggesting that I should look for another church? Frankly, I'm a little shocked so many of you talk about your search for the right church. It would have never occurred to me to do that. I'd feel almost disloyal," she said. "Yet, how much longer can we go and be unfulfilled? It is so hard to pray when your heart is filled with resentment." She lowered her eyes.

"The structure of the House of the Lord is set up by the official church," Phyllis said. "The Father is the head of the house. We can't escape this. If you have a stern, controlling father, then you won't be allowed to grow. Worse still, an overbearing father raises children who can't wait to leave home as soon as they're old enough," she said.

"In a real sense, we are the children living under his roof, and his house rules. As much as we'd like to do something, he has the final say. Let me tell you a story my cousin shared with me some years ago.

"My cousin moved to Japan when her two children were very young. She had a boy and a girl. Her husband, who was unemployed here, got a great job offer teaching English as a foreign language. Everything was going well except for one thing. Whenever they ate at a restaurant or were out in public, her daughter was ignored. All attention was given to the son. It was like she didn't exist. My cousin explained to her daughter that the culture there was different. They talked about it at home. Yet, as she watched the pain it caused her little girl, she knew she could not let it continue. For perhaps, slowly, her daughter would believe that she didn't have any self-worth. She didn't count.

"In the end, as good as the job was, they had to leave. That story had a great effect on me, especially so with our own awareness of the women's issues plaguing the church today. Now, these are only my own personal reflections. But I feel we have a right to share them honestly with one another."

A woman in a blue polyester suit began to speak. She wore a headband to keep her page-boy hair in place. "I'm here as a godmother, and I wish to state that I'm very happy with my church. We have altar boys and I don't see anything wrong with that," she said. "It helps boys to think about becoming priests. I wish the Mass was still in Latin. There's just too many changes in the church today," she said. "I hope this won't hurt anyone's feelings. I just can't understand why women can't see they are important in the church, but they do have their place. I totally disagree with what you're saying. People have to go to the church they belong. Why, you'd create total chaos, having people hopping from one church to another every time they disagreed with something," she finished.

"We should be careful, very careful about what we're saying here," Phyllis replied. "When we talk about searching for a church, we're certainly not saying to jump from one church to another anytime a conflict arises, or something happens that might not be to our liking. What we're suggesting is that you find the House of the Lord where you know both you and your family can grow up to be children who will be allowed to give back their gifts to the family. Children who can grow to be adults in the community and in their faith. Once you find this house, stay. Work through the disagreements, just like in any other family. Just don't stay away. Find the place you belong. There is no right church, only the one that is right for your family."

The woman shook her head in disagreement as Phyllis looked to the next person in the circle. She was a woman who appeared to be in her late 20s. She was alone and sat attentive, but aloof, throughout all of the discussion. She wore a plain brown skirt and a white cotton sleeveless knit shirt. Her brown and white saddle shoes completed the outfit.

"My name's Kathy," she said, matter-of-factly. "I just want to say that I went to church and parochial school my whole life and I have a strong personal relationship with Jesus. I plan to teach my child myself. I feel quite capable of doing that. I don't feel I need church. And while all this friendliness is good, it's not for me, thank you. Nor do I see the necessity of it for faith development," she added.

"That, of course, is your right," Phyllis replied. "I only ask that you reflect on why you have such a strong personal relationship with Jesus. Could it be because you had church all your life while you were growing up? And can that same strong relationship that you know be transmitted to your children without going to church every week? I tried it myself for some time," Phyllis added. "I tried to keep Jesus in our little family, but it didn't work. There always seemed to be something missing in our lives. When I went back to church, I focused on me and Jesus. And unexpectedly, I found Jesus through the community. I hope it will work for you," she said.

"If I could just say one thing," Mike said. "Just the other night, my son Timmy wrote a story and gave it to us. It basically went like this. Timmy wrote that he dreamt he played the lottery. That very night, the numbers he played came out and he was really happy. He was thinking and thinking what to do with all the money when a man knocked on the door who was very poor and had old clothes and nothing to eat. So, Timmy gave him half of all the money he won."

Mike's hand subconsciously reached for his cross, as he paused briefly, holding the cross and cocking his head to one side. "The story ended with the man taking the money and saying to Timmy, 'Bless you.' And Timmy said that made him feel even happier than when he won all that money."

Mike smiled proudly. "I share that story only because I don't think those kinds of feelings would have happened in our family without church. It's things like the food pantry and the box project that teach our boys to think about the poor. And so do their CCD classes and the stories Father tells. My wife and I were never big church givers, and now we tithe part of our income because we know our money is going directly to care for the poor. We talk about this as a family, and it's really changed our lives," he said. "I know we couldn't have done this on our own."

"I'd just like to ask one thing," a woman blurted out. "My name is Anne and I've been coming here for over a year. I'm the godmother for Jim and Katie's baby, Bethany. I hear all of you talking about being part of the church family, and I'd like to ask a question. How do you break into the circle? You all seem to know one another, and it's obvious on Sunday how close people in this community are. I'm a teacher and I feel I have gifts I'd like to return, but how do you get involved? Who do you talk to?" she asked breathlessly. Freckles splashed across her thoughtful, sunburned face and her brown eyes were glistening.

"Well," Kim said, "not too long ago I was trying to figure out how I came to be sitting here every month at these Baptism groups, sharing with you things that others much closer to me have never heard me talk about. I used to be so timid I'd become paralyzed when a teacher would call my name to answer a question."

As she spoke, she rolled some papers she held in her hand. "You're looking at someone who couldn't even call for a pizza!" she confessed, pointing self-consciously to herself. Everyone in the room laughed and she freely joined in, momentarily forgetting herself. Unexpectedly her face blushed as she took a quick breath, shook her head slightly and said, "Oh no, I lost my train of thought." She looked down to her lap. But in a second, her hand rose in the air, allowing everyone to breathe again.

"Oh, I remember now. Jesus is always calling us to him. But we have to answer and take the first step. Then we choose," she emphasized, "whether or not to take another step forward. My first step back to church and Jesus was choosing baptism for my children. But I had to take this same step over and over. It wasn't until the baptism of my third baby that I was ready for another.

"My next step forward was so simple." She continued to roll the paper in her hands. "All I did was ask a question. At one religious education Sunday, I spoke with Gerry about not knowing what the rules were. I felt I couldn't play the game, so to speak, if I didn't know the rules. So many changes had been made while I was away from church that I didn't know what was expected. The next thing I knew I had been asked to join a Serendipity Bible Study Group.

"This step forward was so effortless. All I did was to show an interest." She looked at Anne as she said this. "When asked to join the study, I chose to say yes!" She slapped the rolled-up paper in her hand, her face reflecting her determination.

"When we started doing Baptism this way, with all of us sharing our own faith journey," her eyes made an inclusive sweep across the room, "it originated from a need in the community to welcome new people to our church. I felt a need to share with parents coming to Baptism this sense of community and caring that I have found. Maybe your next step will be as simple as a visit to our playgroup. Or as fun as joining the Holy Stitchers that meet on Monday. Maybe you'd like to join a Bible study or be part of the Children's Liturgy team. All in all, it is up to us whether we choose to keep moving forward—no matter how small the step!" She caught the rolled-up paper with her hand precisely as she said the last word.

"I guess this is a good time to pass out the playgroup newsletter," she continued. "If you're not working days, perhaps you'd enjoy coming to our playgroup that meets on Thursday morning from 9:30 to 11:30. Many mothers who have newborns come just for the company. It's just as much for us as the kids," she joked. "It's a friendly group that gives mothers a chance to get together. We're trying to get fathers to come to playgroup as well, since some of the fathers are home with the children. A few have started coming to the group. This is a great way to meet people in the community and to find out what's happening in church. Beth, Maureen and I are part of it, so you already know someone," she smiled in her friendly manner. "And you don't have to belong to St. Blaise, either. So you can bring a friend, they'll be more than welcome. The details are on the newsletter," she said as she finished passing them out.

Kim sat down and the room became quiet again. Phyllis looked at the next couple in the circle who hadn't yet spoken. The wife looked at her husband in panic. "You don't have to share anything if you'd rather not," Phyllis said. "We've certainly covered a lot of ground tonight. Perhaps you could just introduce yourselves."

The husband caught his wife's eye and quickly began to make the introductions. "My name's Andrew," he said, pointing to himself, "and this here's my wife Alice." He pointed to her. His wife looked at him again. "Oh yeah," he continued, "this is my brother Dan and his wife Ellen." They nodded in turn and certainly all looked too young to have children. They looked extremely uncomfortable.

The woman seated next to them was quick to assess the situation and began to speak. "My name's Kerri," she said in a cultured voice. "This is my husband Robbie. Our close friends Courtney and Joey are the godparents. We moved out from the south two years ago. To tell you the truth, I'm not Catholic. When we got married, we decided to bring up our children as Catholics because of my husband's strong church background." She waved her hand toward him, and he took the cue.

"I'm extremely pleased to have stumbled on this church," Robbie smiled graciously, his perfect white teeth lighting up a handsome face. "After hearing all of you, I wish I could say I thought to go around the area to find the right church for my family. The fact is, we live right across the street. But I can tell you, we'll be coming back," he said.

"My name's Joshua," a young man in a blue print shirt began, "and this is my wife Brianne. The godparents are Jacky and Luke." They smiled comfortably. "The only thing I'd like to say is that I was very involved in church as a kid. We moved out to Bellingham a few years ago after we got married. We live in the complex next door to Robbie and Kerri. When we had the baby, we called our old church to find out about having the baby baptized. That's where I made all my sacraments. They told us that since we didn't belong there anymore, we'd have to call the church where we live. I couldn't understand why we couldn't just go back to our old church, and they certainly didn't seem to have time to explain it to us. So, I must admit, we came here because we had to if we wanted to have our baby baptized. But that's our story," he said, throwing his hands in the air.

"Again," Phyllis said, "just for the record. You really should have your baptism in the church where you will be celebrating your faith. Baptism is us, the church community, welcoming your family into our church family. That's why we have our baptisms during the Sunday liturgy."

She clapped her hands together and said, "I guess we're ready to talk about the actual baptism. I think everyone except Kathy, Peter and Madeline have been here on Baptism Sunday, so we'll go over it quickly.

"Everyone in the community knows that the third Sunday of the month is Baptism Sunday. They'll automatically reserve the first three benches on each side of the church for your families. Please have your entire family sit with you. Also, they are more than welcome to come up when it's time for the baptism. This is especially nice for the grandparents, who probably have never stepped foot in the sanctuary before. I'll be sitting up at the altar, and when Father has finished the homily, I'll get up. That's your signal to come up. Father will ask the babies to bring up the family," she said smiling. "Now you'll all make a wide semicircle. There's seven families, so don't be afraid to spread out right across the altar area. Believe me, the people want to see you.

"Now, the first thing Father will do is anoint the babies. Each time, give Father the full name of the baby and remember to open their garments for the anointing. The anointing is a beautiful tradition of kingship. Your child will be a king in the Kingdom of God, a Kingdom which is now. And to be King in this Kingdom means to learn to be a servant. This is one of the things you will be teaching your children in your role as first teachers in the ways of faith.

"We will then say the baptismal vows together. This is our own opportunity to renew our baptismal vows. You have two choices for the baptism, infusion or immersion, which we call the tub baptism. Infusion is the normal baptism where Father will pour the water over the baby's forehead. Immersion is completely immersing the baby in water. Not the head of course," she added quickly, as she read some of the pictures reflected in the mothers' eyes.

"Water is the symbol of new life, the Exodus experience, coming out of bondage. For me, immersion carries more of the symbol of Baptism. It is the closest we come to the Jordan.

"Also, if you choose immersion, your baby will come in wearing a simple outfit that can come off quickly. The christening clothes will be placed on the altar table. That in itself is special. The new clothes represent their new life in Christ. The early Christians wore a white robe to symbolize this. Also, the feeling of completely lowering your baby in the tub," her hands translated the action, "is a feeling of completely surrendering to the Lord."

"The decision is left up to the parents. One thing to remember is that no one is in a hurry. It is very informal and the people really do enjoy the baptism, especially the children. They'll just be coming up from the children's Liturgy of the Word and they'll sit on the floor in front of the first pew to watch the baptisms. They know every step.

"If you choose immersion, I'll give you a large towel before Mass begins. You can undress the baby while you're up on the altar and wrap the baby in the towel. After the baptism, you dress the baby on the altar table and go back to where you were standing. Then Mike will light the baptism candle from the Pascal candle and give the candle to the godmother to hold. I love the symbol of the light. This is a symbol that grows in importance each year as your child gets older. There are so many young people today who seem to walk in darkness and despair. And yet the children who know Jesus will always have this light in their life.

"I like to mention the godparents' role at this point. The church requires that one of the godparents be Catholic. This is because a godparent's role is to provide the child with a Catholic upbringing, should anything happen to both of the parents. This would be quite difficult if the godparents weren't Catholic. But more than that, the godparents should be a spiritual role model for their godchildren. By going to church themselves, they will be another spiritual connection in the family, teaching their godchild that church is something very important in their lives too. So you do have a role in this baptism, one I'm sure you don't take lightly. It is a great privilege to be asked to be a godparent, one that took a lot of thought on the parents' part. And doesn't it get harder and harder to find people who go to church regularly?" she asked thoughtfully.

"Now where was I? Oh, yes, you just got the candle. I know a lot is going on all during this time. But if you can, try to listen to all that Father is saying about the traditions and the promise you will be making to indeed be the first teachers in the ways of faith.

"Now after this, you'll all be back to your places and you'll hold the baby in the air as high as you can. We'll sing 'Glory to God, Glory' while the whole community claps as a sign of our joy to welcome you to the family. This is the babies' favorite part," she said. "Then you'll be free to sit down.

"We always ask one of the Baptism families to set the table. Would any of you like to volunteer?" she asked. Jim raised his hand immediately. "My children already gave me orders to ask if we could set the table," he said. "Good," Phyllis replied. "That settles that. Now you know, of course, that during the Our Father, we all go out of our benches and hold hands. If your relatives are sitting at the ends of the benches, you might want to remind them of this. Did I forget anything?" Phyllis asked.

"Do the godparents still hold the baby?" Kathy asked.

"I'm glad you mentioned that," Phyllis said. "No, both of the parents hold the baby and everyone touches the baby."

"Should we get there early?" Laura asked.

"No," Phyllis said smiling. "Five of ten should be plenty of time. We have a Bible sharing from 9:00 to 10:00 every Sunday before Mass, and it always seems we get to the height of it when it's time to come up for Mass. Right now we're reading Jeremiah."

There seemed to be no more questions. "If you think of anything else during the week, feel free to call me at the rectory And I always like to add at this point that if anyone here has had a problem with church that would keep you away, please," her eyes pleaded, "don't leave without mending it. This is the most important thing you will ever give your family, so make it work! Now," she continued in a lighter voice, "what have you decided, infusion or immersion? Laura?"

"I think we'll go with the tub," she said, smiling to Mitch.

"We will, too," Jim said. "Direct orders from Cindy. She got to baptize five dolls at one of her First Communion classes, and that's what she wants for her sister." Jim and Katie both chuckled.

"The regular infusion Baptism will do fine for me," Kathy said.

"I think we'll do that, too," Andrew said, after his wife whispered to him.

"Oh, what the heck," Joshua said, "I think we'll go for it, the complete immersion."

Peter and Madeline were still discussing it. Finally Peter said, "I'd rather have the infusion myself, but Madeline wants the tub, so I guess we'll go with that."

"Actually," Kerri said, "we need more time to make our decision. Could I let you know sometime during the week?" she asked.

"Of course," Phyllis answered. "You can call me at the rectory during the day or you can reach me at home evenings. As long as I know before Sunday so I can prepare the tubs." She smiled and looked around the room.

"So, that's four immersions, two infusions, and you'll let me know before Sunday," Phyllis took note. "The immersion baptisms will be first so you'll have time to get the babies dressed while we do the infusions. Could you write down what you chose on the bottom of the yellow Baptism forms?" she asked. "I just want to add that, of course, each baby will have their own tub. Also, please turn the sheet over and write the names and ages of your other children on the back," she directed.

"Speaking of older children," Maureen said to the group as some continued writing on their sheets, "I brought a copy of a letter we wrote for the Children's Liturgy." She held up the papers in her hand. "I knew several of you had older children and you might like to take this home to read how the Children's Liturgy evolved and what we are trying to do. And even if you don't have older children, it's good to know this will be available for your children when the time comes." She passed out the papers.

"We talked about so many things tonight that it probably seems a little overwhelming," Phyllis said. "But there are bulletins at the doors of the church that will keep you updated on all our happenings. And we're always here to answer any of your questions. It's hard to remember everything, which reminds me of something I always try to pass along at our Baptism sharing.

"Baptism is a perfect time to begin the tradition of blessing your children every night before they go to bed," she said. "This was a gift Father gave us when my two children were baptized. You simply make the sign of the cross on their forehead." She turned to Joshua, and touching his forehead, made the sign of the cross saying, "I bless you, Joshua, in the Name of the Father, The Son and the Holy Spirit." You could touch the power it held. "This is a wonderful, rich church tradition that will greatly bless your family. And even though you fight right up till bedtime," she laughed, "your last words to one another before you go to sleep will be ones of peace. Church will give your family many gifts and blessings and many unexpected surprises," she said knowingly.

While they talked the sun had slowly set, leaving the room with a drowsy, relaxed feeling. She knew it had happened. A moment born of the Spirit that would never be fully comprehended by any of them. She engaged each person's eyes for a brief moment before ending the night.

"Tonight was a wonderful sharing, and I hope the beginning of a new relationship together." She held out her hands. "Well, I guess you're free to go. And I'll see you on Sunday." For a moment no one moved.

Kathy was the first one to get up. She quickly handed her paper to Phyllis, nodded, and walked out of the room. Alice and Andrew followed on her heels. "My mom's babysitting so we have to leave," Alice said, escaping any personal dialogue. Phyllis shook their hands warmly. "I look forward to seeing you both on Sunday."

Meanwhile, everyone else had formed in small groups. Joshua and Brianne went over to Phyllis. "I didn't want to say this in front of the group," Joshua almost whispered, "but I was really hurt by the way I was treated by my old church. I grew up there," he said, his blue eyes reflecting a mixture of rejection, hurt and confusion.

"Just think," Phyllis replied, "if you had gone back there for the baptism, chances are that would have been it for church, since it's too far to travel every week. Sometimes Jesus has to close a door to almost force us to open the one we need," she said. To her complete surprise, Joshua bent his head back and laughed heartily. "Are you this optimistic about everything?" he asked. "Yes," Phyllis assured him. "Nothing in our lives is a coincidence, you know. Everything has a reason, a purpose. We just need to discover it."

She reached out her hand and Joshua surprised her again by hugging her. In turn she hugged Brianne and the godparents, Ellen and Dan. But as Dan was leaving, he reached for her hand, speaking as much through his clear gray eyes as the words he said. "You will never know how much this night has meant to me." As he turned to leave, she noticed the small gold earring he wore that seemed to weigh far too heavily on his slight frame.

Joshua's hug had started a chain reaction and everyone hugged one another as they made their way out the door until Maureen, Beth, Mike, Kim and Phyllis were alone again.

"What a powerful night," Phyllis said. "It never ceases to amaze me how every month is so different. It's like the people themselves draw from us the Spirit and the words they need. You can feel it as it builds in the air. I definitely won't sleep tonight," she said.

"And you never know what people are getting out of it," Beth said. "Remember that young man who kept looking around, at the ceiling, at his shoes, everywhere but us, and all of a sudden he started crying?" she said in amazement. "After that night I try not to judge from people's outer reactions what they're thinking or how much they get out of this. If they don't appear to be listening, I look to all of you to get strength," she smiled, "because you just never know what really happens on a Baptism night. Like tonight, Wow!" she exclaimed.

"I felt like we were on fire," Kim said, her blue eyes aflame. "Anne talked to me about the Children's Liturgy and Serendipity. She's really interested. She mentioned about going downstairs after Mass for coffee and donuts next Sunday. I told her I'd ask Jacque to join us. I think after she talks with Jacque she'll decide to join the team."

"Jim and Katie were telling Peter and Madeline about the Religious Education Program," Mike said. "I didn't have to say a word. It's too bad Kathy and that young couple had to leave right away. What were their names?" he asked.

"Andrew and Alice," Maureen supplied. "We'll have to look for them." Yes, they all agreed, making mental notes of all of this.

"I was talking to Laura and Mitch," Maureen reported. "I think they'll be trying the Children's Liturgy for Sara. And I think Laura's going to come to playgroup on Thursday," she said, rubbing her hands together.

Beth was next to join in. "Robbie seemed very interested in everything. With his strong church background, maybe you could invite him to the Serendipity group that will start up in Lent," she said to Phyllis. "Kerri, well, I'm not so sure, though she's certainly friendly enough. Kerri's mother is living with them. Since they just moved, she doesn't know anyone. I'm going to look for them on Sunday and invite them both to the Holy Stitchers. Just from the little bit Kerri said, it sounds like she could use the company. I think it'll be a good way to draw them both into the community."

"I'm concerned about Peter," Phyllis said. "The best part is that they have older children. Jennae's nine and Stacey's five. If they become dancers in the special liturgies or take part in the Christmas Eve pageant, that will be the best way to bring Peter back to the church. Children certainly have the power to work miracles. Joshua and Brianne are a lovely couple. We'll have to especially invite them to games night or a potluck supper. I might try Serendipity for them too. Kathy reminds me a lot of myself. Hopefully, she'll come to the realization that there's something missing in your life when you try to keep Jesus just in your own family. And Andrew and Alice just need time and extra reaching out.

"I don't know what I'd do without you now," Phyllis continued lovingly to the group. "People need to be drawn into the church family. One person simply can't keep track of all these new couples. I don't think I could do it alone again."

"I get as much strength out of these meetings as they do," Maureen said in her humble way. "After a night like tonight, I don't have any doubt about what I want for my family."

"Hey," a voice boomed, coming somewhere from in the church and heading to where they were. "What are you people still doing here?" Father Connolly asked. "Sorry I had to miss it," he said. "What am I saying?" he joked. "You people do better without me. Those people don't need me talking theology at them at this point in their life. How did it go?" he asked.

"We were on fire," Kim ventured boldly from behind a paper that hid her face below her eyes. "They just left a few minutes ago. We had incredible sharing tonight," she said.

"That wouldn't happen if I was here, you know," he said seriously. "They'd be afraid to say what they were really thinking. You people get right to the level you need to be at baptism. You speak to them straight from your hearts. That's what's got to start happening with church," he said, making a sweeping golf gesture with his hands. "Couples teaching other couples. Sometimes the clergy has to get out of the way and let it happen," he said, allowing a sparkle to light up his eyes.

"None of this could happen without you," Maureen said shyly. "Me?" Father said. "You people do it all."

"Kim," Father said in a voice loud enough to halt the conversation that was leading up to the vital role he has in making all this work, "did you tell them how I almost made you cry at your baptism?" His face was soft with unspoken apology. Kim blushed deeply, thinking of how he had actually asked her forgiveness.

"I deserved it," she replied in his defense. "You only asked if I was serious this time. It made me determined to prove you wrong," she said.

"I didn't even know you were hurting until later," he said, putting his hand on her arm. "But priests are trained to ask questions. We Catholics are people with papers," he said. "And I couldn't have been more wrong about you being serious, now could I?" he said, smiling.

"Well," she answered, "since it took the third time around to catch hold, I really could understand your attitude."

"In a way, I'm glad it happened," Phyllis said. "We are planting a seed. Sometimes it takes several attempts, even years to take hold. And we can't expect people to be where we are coming from, we have to go to them. One thing is certain, we'll never get anywhere with negative attitudes," she said gently. "We all learned a valuable lesson from Kim's experience."

"Yes, I did," Father corrected, his hazel eyes twinkling and looking boyishly handsome against the wisdom of his white beard. "You people will make a Christian out of me yet!" he teased in his ever humble, gracious way.

It was 10:00 a.m. Father walked through the church, still not dressed for the 10:00 liturgy. He was quietly greeting people, mentally noting who was new, who was absent. Teaching the community as he did best, through his own gentle example. Saying to us, this is how the liturgy begins. Conversation was taking place throughout the church, as families greeted one another and consciously made an effort to welcome any new families near them. Indeed, Mass had begun.

The Baptism people sat in the first three benches of the church. They looked uncomfortable and conspicuous. Coming home after a long time away does that. In particular, they studied the priest. In this case, a gentle shepherd, dressed simply in a plain white robe, adorned only with a handwoven green embroidered stole from El Salvador.

Their senses took in the community, the openness, warmth, and genuine joy of the family coming together around the table. It wasn't quite like they remembered, yet it triggered a time past when Sunday was special, different from the rest of the week. Perhaps it brought them to remember their own childhood memories of church, stories they had long forgotten. There was so much to consider. For subconsciously, they were in the process of making the most important decision of their lives. Is this a place I want to bring my family once a week?

Out of the seven couples who are there, probably three will return to church immediately on a regular basis. Two of the couples will slowly be drawn back to church, in a one-to-four year timeframe, through letters and invitations, contact with playgroup, or perhaps a second baptism. Two of the couples will not return. This is not for us to understand. "My thoughts," says the Lord, "are not like yours, and my ways are different from yours. As high as the heavens are above the earth, so high are my ways and thoughts above yours."

We have done our part. We have let them know they are special to the family. We have given them the view of the Father who watches in the window for their return. Not with rebuke or conditions, but with the best robe, and open arms for a feast, a celebration upon their return.

As the seven couples raise their babies high in the air, dressed in their new white garments, the community bursts into song and a welcoming applause that says, "Yes, the door of the House of the Lord has been opened to you. Come, be part of the family, we rejoice to welcome you home!"

Playgroup

"In my Father's house are many rooms . . ."
John 14:2

After I had been coming to church here for a few months, I de-cided to introduce myself to Father Connolly," Maureen was say-ing to several mothers from the playgroup. As often happened, the conversation had turned to church.

"My daughter Emily was with me and had been reasonably well-behaved during Mass, though the stress of her good behav-ior was beginning to take its toll," she continued. "But I thought I could risk a quick hello without her losing it all together. I was mistaken. The more I tried to settle her down, the more she revolted. Just as I was about to give my name to Father, Emily raced past us and fell sprawling to the floor. She just missed overturning plants, a music stand, and, possibly, a few people. The thought of pretending that she wasn't mine crossed my mind." Maureen's eyebrows went up and the mothers laughed knowingly. "Well," she went on, "Father Connolly looked at her, smiled and said, 'Isn't it wonderful to see the children so com-fortable with God!' "

"Hah! Comfortable with God!" I thought. "She was out of control! But over time, I realized that the only way kids are go-ing to be comfortable in God's house is if they visit it often, even when they are very young and occasionally unruly."

Playgroup had to be moved when it became too large to con-tinue meeting in one another's homes. Initially, a group of mothers who were members of the St. Blaise community got to-gether once a week to share thoughts, form friendships and en-courage their children in a supervised group play. Yet, so many others began to express an interest and desire for this kind of experience that the group thought of utilizing the church hall once every week. St. Blaise welcomed this mission with open arms.

It was wondrous to see the transition of "five women meeting in each other's kitchen" to "five women emerging as strong leaders in an important ministry." Everything was in place for that to happen. The women had been part of our adult family religious education program for some time and had continued in their own faith journey. Also, they were involved in the first Serendipity Bible group that was offered at our church, a group which targeted people already in ministry, as well as potential leaders in our community. While Serendipity is based on Scripture study, it draws people more into looking at their own personal relationship with Jesus. What plan does He have for their life based on their situations, their gifts and talents. Playgroup seemed to be the perfect opportunity for their ministry to develop.

From a pastoral view, the playgroup was immediately seen as the perfect room in the House of the Lord where our new Baptism families could be plugged into the church family. More important than being able to find out the happenings of the community, the Baptism people would experience church—people loving and caring for one another. There they would begin to sense the warmth of this new family who had welcomed them—the church family. We have many young mothers who come to our food pantry, and we also try to connect them to playgroup.

Everyone who comes to playgroup is asked to fill out an index card with their name, address and children's names. The playgroup newsletter is mailed to all the families. This also allows the core group to personally keep in touch with new families who might need that extra outreach. It is perfect for inviting new people to church activities. Recently, the core group began a Serendipity Bible Study just for interested parents who were part of playgroup. They called everyone on the list. And even those who couldn't join at this time felt a sense of belonging just because they had been invited.

The playgroup newsletter is posted at the public library, and many families have joined who are not members of our church. While church is never intentionally pushed, because playgroup is located in the church hall and the leaders are so filled with church in their own lives, many wonderful opportunities naturally arise where people who have been away from church feel comfortable to ask their questions in this informal setting. Through the positive, joyful conversations that always follow, many families have decided to give church another try. Playgroup proved to be an unexpected way home. It virtually became a "side door" back into the church for many who found the front door had closed to them for one reason or another.

The children, too, often unwittingly became evangelists through their innocent play. Perhaps being in the church triggers off reminders of their own church experiences, and they naturally carry these thoughts into their games. Sometimes, they pretend they are at church, and suddenly you'll hear a little sing-song voice imitating Father's close of every liturgy, "Mass is over, have a pleasant Sunday!"

A child who doesn't come to church regularly might suddenly run up to her mother and ask, "Can I be an angel in the Christmas pageant this year?" Or, "David is going to Vacation Bible School this summer, can I go too?" The children act comfortable in church. Many insist on stopping in for a minute to "say Hi to Jesus." They speak about church like they enjoy being there. They are a wonderful message.

Yet, there is something that goes beyond even the precious conversations that take place. Each of the leaders wears a simple wooden cross. This visible sign is a silent reminder that we are church, and church is the expression of the Kingdom. They represent how church feels—warm, loving and inclusive.

In the arms of playgroup, everyone feels welcomed. There is a conscious effort to notice the newcomers and draw them in. Mothers who have no transportation are picked up for playgroup. Oftentimes, when a mother is sick, another mother will bring her children. Needs are met in the form of babysitting, cooking meals, listening, just being there. Open meetings are held often to encourage people to voice their opinions as well as air their complaints. The women run the group as simply as Jesus commanded: "Love one another as I have loved you." It doesn't happen without a lot of work, desire and determination.

Initially, playgroup "just met" in the church hall. The formation of any new church group is a critical time. Members are seeking to see if they fit in. When the group was in the beginning stages, the leaders of playgroup held several informal gatherings and invited other church leaders to verbalize how they saw the role of playgroup in the parish. Playgroup was talked about as a ministry for all our families with young children, and a valuable resource that was being directly used for the continuation of the Baptism program. Oftentimes, one group does not always see how connected they are to the whole life of the church family.

Two years later, playgroup has confident leaders who are aware of their ministry. They are women with a vision and purpose that goes beyond their own needs. Playgroup has its own place in the church hall. A special storage area was built to house their supply of endless magic and imagination. It is no wonder the children ask everyday, "Is this the day for church playgroup?"

The playgroup has grown and continues to grow weekly. Playgroup is a sign of the times, an encouraging sign of the revival of the family. What better place than church to be there encouraging the family in any way possible?

The family is the divine institution. The church is the larger family. What a family should be can be known through the example of the church family. Granted, the circumstances, activities, and particulars of each family will vary. But as long as the service of God is the main concern, the attitudes of family will be the same: bearing one another's burdens, being responsible for the development of family, and ensuring that every member is welcomed, accepted, and loved.

"Do not be worried and upset," Jesus told them. "Believe in God and believe also in me. There are many rooms in my Father's house, and I am going to prepare a place for you. And after I go and prepare a place for you, I will come back and take you to myself, so that you will be where I am. You know the way that leads to the place where I am going." (John 14:1-4)

And for many, playgroup is just the right room to lead and welcome them home.

Children's Liturgy of the Word

"From the lips of children and infants
you have ordained praise ..."
                                        Psalm 8:1-2

For Christmas two boys had received a beautiful Children's Bible. One evening their mother read the story of Jacob's Flight and Dream. Upon finishing, Ian, the older boy, looked at the colorful illustrated picture showing angels going up and down the stairway, leading up to heaven.

"Mama," he asked, "Why are the angels walking up and down the stairs?" "Well," she explained, "that is the stairway to heaven." "Yes, I know," the boy replied, "but why are they walking up and down the stairs?" "Well," the mother answered patiently, "it is the gate of heaven and it leads to God's House." "I know, Mom," the boy insisted, "but why are the angels walking up and down the stairs?" Thinking quick on her feet, the mother answered: "Well, the angels are God's messengers and they carry his words back and forth to earth."

"Yes, Mom," the boy agreed, "but why are they walking up and down the stairs? They are angels; they have wings!"

What do we do with the children?

For a long time there were conflicting ideas of whether the children should be part of the Mass or if they would benefit more directly from an experience that was geared to their age level. Our main concern was that we wanted church to be a family celebration. We wanted the children to feel they too were an important part of the Mass.

Jacque, a mother with a young daughter, especially pushed to start a small Bible class for the children and to have it during the first part of the Mass so the children would be out during the readings and homily, which was a difficult time for them and their parents. They would come back into church for the offerings and Eucharist. At the time, her daughter was three and she began to feel that she too should be getting something out of the liturgy at church. Many other mothers liked the idea, were interested, and a few offered to help. However, there was also opposition. Many people felt this would isolate the children from the whole church experience.

For a while, the idea was shelved. However, as the years went by, Jacque felt an even stronger call to go forth with this idea. This time she would not give up so easily. She spoke to Father directly, and he was enthusiastic to try it and see where the Lord would lead them.

Soon after that conversation, it was agreed that we would try a Bible class for children over three years of age. The children went into the sacristy as soon as they came into church and stayed until after the collection. Most of the time the children's group was small. A few mothers came to help and Bible stories were read. The children sang, prayed and colored pictures related to the story of that particular Sunday.

Thus was the beginning of the weekly children's educational program, known to some as the "little piece of rug school." Every child was given his/her own square of carpet to sit on, hence the name. It became as much a supervised activity period for the younger children as it was a tool for religious education.

Things continued this way until 1990 when Gerry, our DRE, learned of a Children's Liturgy seminar in Boston. She opened this to the people involved in the liturgy program, and Jacque and two of the other mothers decided to go. What they brought home was the beginning of our Children's Liturgy program that we have today.

Webster defines liturgy as "A prescribed rite for a public religious service: ritual." The children's liturgy is a ritual celebration of the Word. As each Mass begins, the children stay with their families and sing the opening song together. We learned that it is better for the children to join the community in prayer and song at the beginning of Mass in order to recognize that they also belong to God's family. Then, when it is time for the Liturgy of the Word, or the Sunday readings from the Bible, Father gives the children's lectionary (or book of readings) to the person who is leading the children's group that day, and asks them to share the "Word" with the children. He or she leads the children in procession to our room downstairs, which was built for the children when we began our new children's liturgy. One of the children accompanies the leader in the procession and carries down a candle.

The logistics of getting the children downstairs and then back upstairs without disrupting the service can be difficult. Also, there is a large range of ages and differing levels of understanding, attention spans, etc. So the leaders of the program have asked the community to:

Remind your children, when going downstairs, not to rush ahead of the leaders. The minister leaving the altar should be the first one to the back of the church. Remind your children that the liturgy has a purpose, and they should pay close attention. It's not a break from the liturgy upstairs, it's the children's liturgy. If your children go up to the altar following the liturgy, be sure they understand that they should sit quietly. Also, if they should leave the altar prior to the handshake of peace, they should not return to the altar. "One trip to Jerusalem," as Father says. Remind them that some folks prefer a quiet service, and they should not be running or talking as they go up or downstairs, or up to the altar. All ages are welcome, and if you are uncertain whether your child is too young, feel free to accompany him or her the first time down. Ages range from two to about ten. During our time with the children, we center our celebration around the Liturgy of the Word. We read with the children the same readings that the adults have upstairs and help them to make a connection between the Gospels and their own lives. The language in the Scripture readings is somewhat changed to accommodate the children's level of comprehension, and we sometimes let the children dramatize the gospel to help them enter into the story itself. After the readings we always ask the children what they heard and have a brief discussion. We also worship with the children through music, with a song at the beginning of our celebration and singing the responses before the Gospel. Also, we take the special intentions of the children, which provides an opportunity for the ministers to see what the children are concerned about, and what's on their minds on a given Sunday.

With the liturgy, our intent is to bring His word to the children of the parish, and to present it so that they can understand

and enjoy it. We say that this is our intent because we are neither teachers nor Bible scholars, though many of us have begun Bible study to further our own knowledge of Scripture. What we hope to impart is that our daily actions—what we do, how and why we do it, how we feel about the people around us—all these things are taught in the Gospel, and are significant in His plans for us. Our daily actions are what define us, and we hope to show the children that there is some meaning in everything we and they do. A lot of this is translation of what the Gospel says into terms and experiences that the children can relate to. This always provides a challenge, but also provides rewards when you can see that some of the children have made a connection between the readings and their own lives.

Parents, too, see the connection and are very excited about this learning experience that enables their children to encounter Jesus through His words at their own level. We see more and more children attending the Children's Liturgy of the Word. The liturgy room is usually at capacity. The teams of mothers and fathers who lead the liturgy have evolved into seven groups of adults who take turns every two weeks to provide the atmosphere and opportunity to allow children their own prayer. For Children's Liturgy is not a class, it is truly a time of worship by the children where they communicate, speak, and listen to the Lord.

Religious Education

*"Remain united to me, and I will remain united to you.
A branch cannot bear fruit by itself; it can do so only if it
remains on the vine. In the same way, you cannot bear
fruit unless you remain in me."*

John 15:4

Every Saturday when we were kids, our cousins would come over and we'd play in our cabins in the woods. At the edge of the woods there was a long straight path. If you followed it and went over a small hill, you'd find Robert, Kathy and Mary's cabin. They were the oldest. Their cabin was a grassy area that was always in the sun. They simply took four long tree branches and laid them across other trees to form a perfect square.

Now if you followed the path and took a right, you'd find Tommy and Jacky's cabin. They were the youngest. Tommy and Jacky had raked their cabin to bare earth. They had stones completely outlining their cabin, and in the middle was a perfectly arranged stone fireplace with little branches set in place for their fire. Michael and I were the middle children. If you wanted to find us, you'd have to look, because we moved cabins every week. We never could decide which spot was the prettiest.

Some years ago, when my two children were little, these cousins came back for a family reunion. They're spread out all over the country. Well, we started talking about the old days and, of course, the cabins came up.

They couldn't wait to tell my kids how Michael and I used to move very week. And we talked about the time Robert was pretending to be a wolf and a real German shepherd got loose from a neighbor's house. That dog had to be bigger than any wolf. We all remembered that. And we couldn't believe how good Robert was acting, until the dog came leaping down the path after him, and we just nearly escaped by throwing ourselves under the Pass.

The Pass was this enormous rock we used to scale up. We all had one of those perfect rocks when we were growing up. You know the kind. You can barely get up one side, but once you do, you feel like you're indeed king of the mountain.

And then there was Blueberry Hill. Blueberry Hill was this wide mound in the woods. It was covered with the most beautiful blueberries you've ever seen. I remember how we had to reach up to pick them.

Well, when we got home, the kids asked me if Blueberry Hill was still there and if I could find it. Of course I could find it, I told them. Every detail of that woods was clearly etched in my memory.

So we set out one Sunday to find Blueberry Hill. Sure enough, there was the path. The minute my feet started on it, I broke into an easy gallop. We always rode our horses on those paths, you never walked. Soon we reached the spot where Blueberry Hill should have been. Granted, there were the most beautiful blueberry bushes one could imagine. But they were only this high, just about waist level.

And that big mound? Well, you could hardly tell there was an incline. But the clincher was when I saw the rock, the Pass I could hardly scale. What could have happened? Surely the rock must have sunk into the ground after all those years! It just couldn't have been that small. Now, my kids thought the whole place was great, just like I had described. But I couldn't believe how different it all looked to me now. I guess when you're little you can only see things from "waist high."

It got me to start thinking about other childhood memories. Memories I had of Jesus and the church. Were things as big as I had imagined? What would it feel like if I could return? But mostly, would it always "look" the same to me if I didn't go back to see it through adult eyes?

Blueberry Hill had taught me a valuable lesson. If, as an adult, I didn't go back to the sacraments, to the "confession line," to the church teachings, to Scripture, I would always have a view from "waist high." There was a path back, and that path was through adult religious education.

Religious Education Program

- Where we were and how we got to where we are now
- This is part of a presentation that was given by Gerry, our DRE, during one of the adult sessions of our Religious Ed program.

"About 18 years ago, the bishops came out with a Pastoral directing that we do adult education. We took a look at our parish and said, yes, we're kind of doing that, because we're involving parents in preparation for First Communion, and yes, we're involving parents in preparation for First Penance. But that was basically all we did for adult education. It wasn't long before we came to the conclusion that's not really what they meant.

"We looked closer at the documents from Vatican II:

> 'Parents have conferred life on their children, they have a most solemn obligation to educate their offspring. Hence, parents must be acknowledged as the first and foremost educators of their children. Their role as educators is so decisive that scarcely anything can compensate for their failure in it. For it devolves on parents to create a family atmosphere so animated with love and reverence for God and men that a well-rounded social and personal development will be fostered among the children. Hence, the family is the first school of those social virtues which every society needs.'

"Also, the National Catechetical Directory tells us that:

> 'Catholics have a right to look to their parishes to carry out Christ's mission by being centers of worship, preaching, witness, community, and service. At the same time, parishioners have reciprocal duties of involvement and support toward their parishes. Maturity of faith obviously rules out the neglect of one's duties as a parish member.
>
> Every parish needs a coherent, well-integrated catechetical plan which provides opportunity for all parishioners to encounter the gospel and respond by fostering community and giving service.'

"With that in mind, we took a look at our program and what was happening with our programs. At that time we had a home program. One of the first things we noticed when we did this was that we had taken on the parent's responsibility. We had left the parents with nothing to do except drop their children off. We had taken the very thing away from the parents that they were directed to do.

"We also noted we didn't have enough teachers. In a home program you only have enough room for how big somebody's house is who is willing to teach. And as we got up into the fifth grade, the sixth grade, and teenagers, well, no one wanted them in their homes. First grade okay, but teenagers, they weren't so sure.

"One thing that was very obvious was that there was a total lack of control as to what material was being presented to the children. Yes, everybody had a book. Then we found out maybe half the teachers were using the books. Some didn't like the book, they didn't know how to use the books. So that was the end of the books, other than the kids carried them back and forth to class.

"Essentially, we had a babysitting service. Fine, people could drop their kids off, and they were being taken care of for another hour or so. Parents could rationalize that their children were learning religion. Yet we found that the majority of the children who were in our program didn't attend liturgies. Their parents didn't even come to church. There was no connection except this one hour a week.

"Children learn what they live. And in one hour a week, they're not living very much as far as religion goes. So we said, 'What can we do?' We prayed about it. We asked, 'How did Jesus teach? Who did Jesus teach?' And the more that we prayed about it, the more it became obvious. Jesus loved little children. He always welcomed them. But he never taught them. He taught the adults. What kind of a statement were we making to the parish at that time? We were telling the parish very emphatically that the most important thing in our parish was the children. Because this is who we were teaching, the children. And as far as anybody else was concerned, you were sort of second to what was happening in the classes.

"After much consideration, we began the program that we have. (Most of the people who would have objected had already left the parish when we began our home program.) We meet monthly, usually on the first Sunday of the month. Children are in classes. While the children are in classes, the adults meet in the church hall. Usually, we try to have the same theme. For example, last year, creation was picked as something to begin with in the classes. In the adult session, we talked about the creation of this program. We felt it was time, due to the fact that numerous new families have joined the parish and are not familiar with a family program.

"We began with the Paulist program, which is a very set program. When the program initially began, the children were in classes, then families met together and did a family project. Liturgy followed. We went a couple of years with this format, then decided to have liturgy before the program. This was much better, as the liturgy set the tone for what was to follow.

"One of the things that we got the most static about in the program was the family sessions. There were so many people participating that it just was always out of hand. We never seemed to accomplish anything because the children were so excited from coming out of classes that they couldn't settle down. The parents also felt they didn't want to do a child's activity. So we let go of that and decided to concentrate of what was happening.

"Every year, at the end of our program, the teachers sit down and evaluate the program. At the last adult session, everyone is asked to comment on the program. Then we sit down and evaluate what we have done this year. Have we met all of the criteria that we hoped to meet during the year? Have we accomplished what we wanted to accomplish?

"Each year we end up making changes, because each year there's somewhere else we can see we need to improve. It should be that way. What we started with 18 years ago should not be where we are today. Our parish has changed. Our people have changed.

"Today, we have classes for 3-year-olds. This year we have a separate class for 4-year-olds. A separate class for 5-year-olds and a separate class for kindergarten. The reason that we label them that way is that some of the children in kindergarten will be 5 and some will be 6 years old. But what constitutes the difference is the ones who will be going to school. Though it doesn't make a difference the first month of the program, about three months down the road those who will be going to school will be in a different place than those who are not yet in school.

"We have classes for grades 1 through 6. We moved our teenagers out of the program. One of the complaints we had about the teenagers in our program, and every year we had the same complaint, (and anyone who has the same type of program that we use, whether it be a home program or they meet in the hall once a week for an hour, has the same complaint) was that our teenagers are losing it—they're not with us. What happens is that it takes the teacher an hour to break through all the social barriers, the peer pressure, and the garbage that the children bring in with them. Things like: I don't want to be here, and I don't like this, and no matter what you say, I'm not going to listen. Then, after an hour, you finally cut through all this and they start listening and it's time to leave. They come back the next week and they're right back where they were before they left. When we had the monthly program, the same thing happened. We were just wasting their time. And no matter what we tried, we couldn't seem to improve it. That's when we started with our retreat programs.

"We base our retreat programs on peer ministry, where we have teenagers in our parish who have made Searches. We break our kids into small groups of maybe four or five. They sit at a table with four or five in the group, and we have a teenager sitting in a group who is part of this peer ministry. We have an older student, usually a student who is in college, as the rector of these retreats. What happens is, as the rector gives a talk or one of the table leaders gives a talk, they talk about it at their table. Then you have the teenagers telling the other teenagers how they live their life with Jesus. How they found Jesus, where they can share Jesus. They are comfortable with this. Some of the feedback that we've received from the teenagers who are in these programs is that they think we should do it more often than we do. They enjoy coming. Oftentimes they're not ready to leave at the end of the day. They would like to stay and do a little more.

"This year we are also offering a learning experience for our 7th and 8th grade classes. This is optional and is run by the youth minister during the regular monthly class time. We've had two sessions so far and most of the kids in our program have freely attended them. We have had a youth minister full-time now for two years. She has begun a weekly Junior C.Y.O., in addition to the C.Y.O. Since most of the kids are in the Junior

C.Y.O., the social barriers are no longer there to break down. Also, she has a wonderful working relationship with the kids that allows a one-hour session to be extremely fruitful. The parents who attend the adult session are glad to have their children in this newly-formed class. However, our main concern is how and if this will affect our all-day retreat programs.

"As far as what happens in the classes? We have guidelines that come from the Archdiocese as to what grade level what material should be available. The teachers have the material that is available for that age or that grade they are teaching. We go according to the guidelines of the Archdiocese and we also use material from books that have been put out. The lesson plans that the teachers receive oftentimes are composed of maybe 3 or 4 different books that are put together to make up one lesson. Our classes go really long. They are really almost 2 or 3 times as long as if we had a weekly program and the kids were dropped off at someone's home. Because of that, it's a big advantage where you want to deliver the message of who Jesus is, but you also want to get in the service aspect. You're able to do that because we can overlap many different themes and topics so that we can tie things together. Also, the children get more of a sense of where everything is.

"The greatest advantage we have found with the program is that we have parents who are really interested in what's happening with their children, and follow along with their children's lives. The parents are learning how to prioritize their time and give to their children what their children need most. The monthly home activity package that each family receives provides parents with helpful information and activities to do that will reinforce what their children have learned in the lesson plan that month.

"The program has also allowed us to develop a strong sense of community within our parish. Never is this more evident than when a call goes out for a need for something. The response is immediate in the community.

"When people come to our parish for liturgy, one of the comments that we always get is, 'We feel like we're part of a family rather than that we're attending a service.' A lot of that has developed out of our parish education program because we do so much sharing together as adults. While there are people who sit in the discussion groups and perhaps never openly communicate, they are still fully participating because they are listening to what's going on. They are comfortable with that, being part of hearing what everyone else has to say. We have small groups so that things can be talked through. And if it's a big enough problem, it can be addressed on a large enough scale.

"One of the advantages that we've found is that we have enabled families to pray together in ways that the families can take a look at their needs and they can meet the needs they have. We've also enabled families to come to more a sense of reading the Bible together.

"And in all of our classes, all through the years leading up to that, we do a lot of Bible study with them. The Bible is the only book used for Confirmation. In fact, many of our teenagers in this parish read the Bible everyday. Many parents don't read the Bible today because that's not something they were taught when they were growing up.

"One of the things that we see is that we're giving children what they need most—parents who are role models. Parents who are living a life in which they are responding in faith to the call of ministry that each one of us has because of our baptism.

"Some of the things that have developed directly because of this program is what's happening with our Children's Liturgy of the Word Program, parish clean-up day, the food pantry, Summer Vacation Bible School, the Serendipity Bible groups, expanding our C.Y.O., and our sacrificial giving program. We've developed a parish that is ready to respond biblically when we're asked to support a parish."

But perhaps of greatest importance is the vehicle adult religious education provides for the community to address issues, discuss matters of concern, and grow in faith together. To experience Jesus and the church from new heights, through adult eyes.

Catholic Schools

Addressing the matter of adult religious education would not be complete without including the issue of Catholic schools. This is of great concern to most parishes and is an issue which we have given careful thought, prayer, and reflection. In the end, we felt as a parish that we cannot participate in supporting Catholic schools.

We cannot embrace any plan that cites schools as a way of preserving Catholic education. It is our feeling that educational and formative Catholic values should be channeled directly through our own church religious education programs. Catholic schools, oftentimes, undermine adult education. It is adults who must first be educated in their faith if the children are to experience church at all. You cannot send a child to "learn religion" if that child is not living that faith in their own homes. We are told that we retain 10% of what we hear, 12% of what we see, 40% of what we read and 90% of what we do. Church is not something we learn about. We have to be church.

As a parish we need an emerging laity. We need to develop programs on the local level to develop the lay leadership. Catholic schools will not be able to meet this need. If our religion was presented through church, through strong faith communities, there should be and would be no need for Catholic schools. We cannot participate in taking resources from the parish for the support of Catholic schools. The funds that would be realized from this could then be directed to the "orphan, the widow, the stranger and the foreigner among us," which is the main directive of collecting the tithe, according to Scripture. Furthermore, we must be ever aware that Catholic schools allow a parent to rationalize away one's own faith responsibility. How can parents fulfill their baptismal promise to be "the first teachers in the ways of the faith," when their own faith journey ends with Confirmation?

At this moment, America needs the Catholic Church to be a prophetic voice. Obviously the Spirit of God would have us see that every single child of God must have everything she/he needs to live a full human life. A basic need for every child of God is that she/he will have all of the education that is necessary and under God has a right to. A prophetic voice has to proclaim this.

We cannot support at this crucial moment in our unjust society suburban Catholics protecting their children from public education. We have to be the leaders in this country for making education the best for everyone. We are praying for a prophetic voice on behalf of all children.

Catholic schools are an alternative education. Because the churches and parents do not have authority over children, public schools must deal with health matters, race, sex education and other issues which are causing the crises in public schools. All of this is intensified by the explosion of knowledge in our time. Public education can be turned around and renewed. Perhaps we should be part of the renewal instead of constructing an alternative system.

First Communion—A Parish Celebration

There is a sturdy string hung along the walls going down both sides of the church. On each side are 17 perfectly-spaced brown paper bags clipped to the string with a clothespin. There is a sheet attached to the front of the bag with a picture of one of our First Communion children displayed. The sheet contains delightful information that the child shares with the community. Such as, "If I had one wish to make for me it would be . . ." And, "If I had one wish to make for the whole world it would be . . ."

At the bottom of the sheet is a space for a parish member who would like to adopt this child as their friend. There is also space for the parish member to share something about themselves.

After Mass on Sunday, families walk around the church learning about our First Communion children, and adopting one for their own. Usually one or more families adopt a child. And many members of the community drop treasures in all the bags. Stickers, balloons, pencils, notes, bookmarks, pins, gum and other imaginative gifts are placed in the bags for several weeks.

One of the mothers shared her daughter's reaction to the whole experience. "I can't tell you how surprised and how much it meant to my daughter when she got home and opened her bag. But it surprised me even more to see that people had taken time to write to her, to sign their name on bookmarks and cards. It made her feel so special and aware that so many people she didn't even know knew her. She couldn't wait to come to church the following week."

The theme for First Communion this year was "Changed By His Love." The program began in February and the children, at that time, placed caterpillars on a large wooden cross in the front of the sanctuary. In March the children made and replaced these caterpillars with cocoons. In April, when they made their First Communion, the cocoons mysteriously "turned" into butterflies.

The first meeting of the First Communion Program is just for the parents. All of our programs involve family and are geared to adult education. The family is the primary and fundamental source of the child's development. Thus it is even more important that the adults be transformed by this experience than the children. By the time the First Communion Program is finished, the parents have learned what Eucharist means.

If a family did not plug into the church at the time of Baptism, then in many cases First Communion will be their "second knock at the door." If a child is making his/her First Communion, the family also has to be enrolled in our family religious education program. This is another opportunity to plug families into church life. Having the parents involved is the key to making this happen.

The first meeting for adults begins with a Bible reading, "Jesus Feeds Five Thousand." They are brought into the story through a series of questions. Where are you in the story? What are you wearing? Can you hear Jesus from where you are standing? The crowd is important. Have your children been in the crowd for a while? Are they comfortable? Are you willing to bring them closer if they are curious?

The theme and the program itself is then explained. The program is a combination of domestic church and parish life. Emphasis is placed on what happens in the home. A filmstrip, Living Eucharist, is shown and after the film they break into small groups to talk about their experience of First Communion and what they want for their child.

The last question focuses on setting priorities. The church's role is to teach children to talk to God. It is the parents' responsibility to teach their children formal prayers. To realize that the community and their own actions will help their children in learning what Eucharist should mean.

The three meetings that follow will include the Wide Game, a Mass Demonstration and the Sunday Party. For the Wide Game, the parents and the children meet in church and experience church hands-on. They are divided into six groups and during the course of the evening visit six "stations" that are set up in the church. They baptize five dolls. They try on the priest's clothes and learn what all the colors mean. They go in and out of the confessional box, and listen to a story about forgiveness. They play a community game to learn about trust. They set the altar table, and talk about how we celebrate the important things and people in our lives: birthdays, weddings, etc. In the same way, we celebrate Jesus in our midst through the Eucharist. They are both nervous and excited to taste the bread for the very first time in their life.

This is a night to make The House of the Lord familiar. And invariably, it is the parents who ask the questions, questions that they have held onto for years and never had a chance to ask. This night is one of the most teachable moments for the adults. It is also a night that draws on the strong lay leadership that has developed. For example, one of the leaders of the Baptism program is there to present the Sacrament of Baptism, etc.

Next is the Mass demonstration. For this, Father meets upstairs with the adults. He shares the meaning of the Mass in detail while the children meet downstairs with Gerry, the DRE, Joyce, who has coordinated the First Communion Program for several years now, and one of the teachers from the Children's Liturgy of the Word. The children share the Mass at their level.

Last is the Sunday Party. A filmstrip is shown. People meet in the same groups that they were in during the Wide Game. At the end of the Wide Game, they planned what each family would bring for the Sunday Party. Pictures of the children are taken at the Sunday Party.

During each session, papers are sent home with the families that further involve the parents in the program. The music people are preparing special music for the liturgy. The meditation this year will be: "If I Were a Butterfly." And several afternoon practices are scheduled for the children since they will each be part of the Mass celebration, whether it be reading, setting the table, or taking up the collection.

First Communion will be celebrated during our 10:00 liturgy. Everyone in the parish will try to attend this celebration to show their support and share this important sacrament with our young children. We are brothers and sisters who hear the same Word, ask each other's peace, and break the same bread. Family sharing within the larger church family. And in the end, through the community sharing of the sacrament of First Communion, we will all have been "Changed by His Love."

The Sacrament of Penance—A Change of Heart

Families are spread throughout the darkened church. One by one, each member in the family reaches for a thin pencil and a small white piece of paper that is at the end of all the benches. Faces are in deep reflection as the pencil struggles to put into words what has broken their relationship with Jesus.

Many of the faces are familiar since this celebration has become a tradition that most of the community looks forward to. This is our beautiful Christmas Penitential that is celebrated each year on the Monday before Christmas week. Most families come to the Penitential as a result of having been a part of the First Penance program that involves both the children and the parents, mostly the parents.

Like the First Communion Program, the First Penance Program begins with a Bible reading, John 8:2-11—The Woman Caught in Adultery. The people are brought into the story. How soon would you pick up a stone? Where would you be in the crowd?

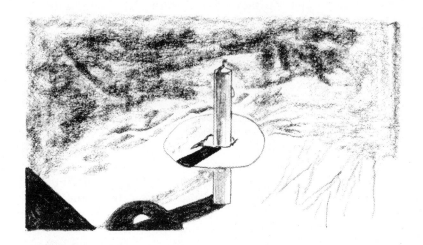

Sin deals with relationships; we are not dealing with giving a theological answer to a question. Parents need to be in touch with where they are at. No one is perfect and we need to realize this. Confession is only a small part of the Sacrament of Reconciliation. The sacrament means to walk together again, to be reconciled with Jesus. It goes beyond the personal and into the social dimensions.

The Penance Program begins in October. There are eight weeks until the Celebration of the Sacrament of Reconciliation— there are eight lessons in the books. The parents are responsible for doing one lesson each week, along with one activity which provides physical signs to see around the house. An example of an activity might be using a felt heart that is sown like a pocket. The parents talk about what kind of a heart you have now. Is it hard like a rock or soft? What kind of a heart does Jesus expect us to have? The child can feel how flat and hard the heart is in the beginning. Each time the child acts unselfishly, either within the family or in school or within the community, the child can place a piece of cotton in the heart. This is a way to physically see how a heart can change and become soft. On Christmas Eve the heart can be placed on or in the manger, or hung on the tree.

It is important for the parents to be preparing the children for this sacrament since they will help their children make moral decisions for the rest of their lives. As such, the parents attend four meetings, with the children attending only the last one.

The program begins with parents discussing their experience of the sacrament and expressing what kind of experience they want for their child. Through the four meetings they learn about the stages of moral development their children are going through. If they have any problems or questions pertaining to using the book, they can seek help at the meeting.

At the last meeting, the parents meet downstairs in the church hall and Mary Ann takes the children upstairs. She reads the story of the prodigal son from the Bible. From Archbooks she reads *The Boy Who Ran Away*. And she shows a modern-day filmstrip of the prodigal son as he would be today. The children go in and out of the confessionals and learn about going to confession face-to-face. They are taught what an examination of conscience is and what they need to think about. They are given the format to use for confession. The Act of Contrition is in the back of the books for the parents to teach them at home.

It is wonderful to see that the children are not afraid of confession. They begin by saying one good thing about themselves. They are not concerned with lists of sins. They truly are learning to talk to Jesus, that Jesus is their friend. He is the loving Father.

This too is what the parents are learning in their last session. Most have fears and memories to overcome about confession. So the last night of the program, Father comes to address sin and what sin is. Three or four people from the community also come to this meeting to share their good experiences of confession with the other parents. This is a very important meeting where people ask questions like, "What ever happened to mortal and venial sins? Do I have to go to confession before I receive Eucharist?" etc. The questions often reveal a waist-high view of the sacrament. Many times fear and bad experiences have kept people from enjoying this sacrament for years. This Penance program is a path back to experience the Sacrament of Reconciliation with new eyes and a change of heart. Our penitential celebration grows each year and the children are part of this wonderful tradition. They are seeing parents who also feel the need for reconciliation and a change of heart. If adults are challenged and feel their own faith is being challenged through vibrant sacrament programs, they will come.

The evidence was there in the full church. One by one, people dropped their "sins" in a huge urn that was in the front of the church before they made their way to the priest. People consciously turning back to Jesus. People going beyond personal, reaching into community, affecting society. Each person bringing a light into the world. Joining their voices to fill the air with "Joy to the World," a sound the world so desperately waits to hear. A song sung from soft hearts.

Confirmation—*Sacramentum*

The Confirmation program begins the night of our December Parish Penitential Celebration. After the candidates sign up for the program, they join the parish in the celebration of the sacrament. It is truly a symbolic way to begin a program which helps the candidate to focus on who they are as a person, what their values are, how they base their decisions, and how all this fits in with the Kingdom and what Jesus expects of them.

The candidates, who begin the class as sophomores, meet for weekly classes every Monday until the end of May. Classes resume in September and end just before Confirmation, which is usually held the first week in December. Besides the classes, the young people are required to attend four all-day retreats, which are based on peer ministry. Our Confirmation program tries to pre-evangelize our youth. They are treated as adult members of the parish, held accountable for themselves, and given the responsibility that goes along with that, including doing a service project.

One of the boys in the class had a particularly difficult time finding a project. It just seemed that nothing suited him. After anguishing about it for some time, he decided to talk to one of the adult leaders. "What do you enjoy doing?" the leader prompted. He thought a second. "Well, I love to skate," he answered. "I bet there is some kid in your neighborhood who would like to skate but has no one to take him," the leader suggested. His face lit up. "There's a little boy who lives in back of my house who would love to go skating," he answered. "You mean you can do something you like and it counts as a service project?" he exclaimed in amazement.

The teens are amazed about many things concerning Confirmation. They don't expect the bonding that slowly happens during the year, the sense of belonging, of trusting one another. In fact, many of the teens say they'll miss Monday night, and maybe it wouldn't be so bad if they just continued to meet as a group.

The theme for Confirmation is "Mission to Love." The only book used for Confirmation is the Bible. And at the first meeting, the whole theme of Confirmation is revealed in the reading from John about Nicodemus. "I tell you the truth, no one can see the kingdom of God unless he is born again . . . Unless he is born of water and the Spirit. Flesh gives birth to flesh, but the Spirit gives birth to spirit."

As they continue in their preparation for the sacrament, they will read the Gospels, Jesus in the New Testament, but curiously they will not find the word "sacrament" in the Bible. Sacrament is a very interesting word that the Church uses to describe all our wonderful celebrations. Yet, sacrament is a secular word. It is the old Latin word *sacramentum*, which was the oath that soldiers in the Roman Army made to the emperor. The soldier would swear an oath of total allegiance to the emperor, declaring himself willing to go anywhere, to do anything, and to die if necessary for the Emperor.

Confirmation. An oath of total allegiance to Jesus Christ the King. A renewal of our loyalty, our commitment to the Kingdom. When the Church was looking for a word to describe our most sacred traditions, she knew that a secular word must be chosen. For in her wisdom, she was telling us that our *Sacramentum*, our oath of allegiance to the Lord, must be taken out into the world.

Marriage

"When I was 19, I was quite a romantic and pretty sure I had marriage all figured out. The first year would be the best. That would be the height of our relationship, the honeymoon. And every year after that would go downhill." She laughed at herself. "I pictured where we'd live. We'd live in a white cottage at the edge of the woods and there would be lilacs at the front door. Every evening at dinner, we'd have fresh flowers and candles on our table. I'd dress in long flowing gowns and each day would be new and exciting.

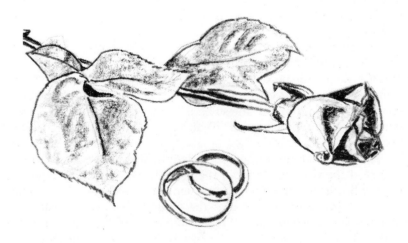

"We ended up living in a very hot third-floor attic apartment. Instead of candles and flowers, there were diapers on the table. And I discovered something strange in the years that followed. I discovered that the first year of our marriage was not the best. In fact, the first year was the hardest—it was indeed paper, just like they say. It was so delicate, so easily torn. We were two people deciding how much we wanted to give to the other.

"But each time one of us gave, the other one wanted to in return. And we found that's how love grows, until you find that each is living for the other. Many nights we stayed up worrying about the children. We sacrificed for them and for each other. And slowly that paper relationship turned to tin. Each year that followed, our relationship grew stronger as we learned to bend and grow together, because we wanted to. The love became as delicate and refined as china. We could walk into a room and speak to each other without the need for words. Our love had been tested in the fire. And something even more unexpected happened. The diapers were replaced by the candles and the wild flowers we picked from the woods at the edge of our house where lilacs grew by the door.

"Each day was new and exciting and our love was more romantic than ever before. Now we understood how to love and exactly what made the other person happy. I am not even jealous anymore, something I never would have believed possible at 20. Even gray hair and wrinkles hold no threat. You know something? Every year is better still, just the opposite of what I had envisioned. Each day we become closer to reaching the gold together.

"I had the same kind of feeling, the same kind of expectations when it came to my relationship with Jesus. When I came back to Him, no longer a child, I thought the first year would be the best, that would be the height of our relationship together. And it wasn't. The first year of my relationship with Jesus was paper. It was so fragile, so easily broken. I didn't really know Him. I didn't know if I wanted to change, to bend, to become one.

"Then the sacrifice came. Those mornings when I forced myself to get up because He was calling. And it was always those moments when it was the hardest that I'd feel Him talking just to me. I'd feel His arm on my shoulder. Suddenly I found myself asking Him what He wanted out of our relationship, instead of telling Him what I wanted. Slowly, but just as real, I felt that paper relationship with Jesus turn to tin.

"Each year that relationship grew stronger as our love was tested and refined in the fire. I realized a relationship is a two-way street. One person can't make it work alone. And this is true of Jesus.

"I left behind the jealousy of what the world has to offer, and found it has nothing to compare with His love. Growing old is beautiful, knowing that I'll be reaching the silver with Him. And on that last day, I can actually picture Jesus finally removing the veil that keeps my eyes from completely seeing His glory. On that day, I will behold the vision of His face and we will celebrate the gold."

With her softly-lilting accent, Phyllis smiles as she tells of the last words of priestly advice she received at the close of nine months of Catholic instruction to get married in the church, "Keep his slippers by the fire and he'll never go out at night!"

Phyllis left her home in Scotland after she and Andy were married. Certainly there was much for a young wife to adjust to, not the least of which was the lonesomeness that enters a heart away from family. When they had their own children, they came back to church. Phyllis warmly describes the memory, "We felt like we had come home, we never knew what we had been missing!"

Phyllis and her husband Andy have been running the marriage program for 15 years. One of the reasons they chose this ministry was to share honestly with young couples what to expect in the early years of marriage. But, foremost, to stress the importance of church in the couple's lives.

Over the years they have learned that marriage is not generally a time when couples return to church. They have just left families of their own, and now want a nest egg for two. They want to shut the world out, at least for now. After the wedding, many of the couples move to a new location. The Sacrament of Marriage is a time for the church to be there for the couple with all her love and warmth. It is a time to sacramentalize their marriage.

The first night Phyllis and Andy meet with the couple, they plan the actual wedding. They have found that this allows the couple to relax. They help them select the readings. They explain the rich traditions of the church like the candle ceremony, traditions that bring Jesus to the center, making Him the foundation for the marriage vows. At the end of the evening, the couple leaves with a workbook, *Perspectives on Marriage.*

The second meeting is a sharing on relationship, as to what a couple might expect in the first years of marriage. It is a surprise for most couples to hear that the first years are the hardest and everyone has their problems. This is a critical time of adjustment, where commitment and communication are the keys to making a marriage work. Constant open dialogue about the smaller things that bother you, like squeezing the toothpaste in the middle, will save major outbursts that are inevitable when all these little things are held inside until everything explodes. It is good to realize that these are common feelings that all couples have to go through. Four years is a kind of turning point in a marriage. By then the honeymoon and the infatuation is over. Marriage is hard work, a good relationship does not just happen. And if Jesus is the foundation of the marriage, there will be a source of strength for the couple to draw on.

Phyllis and Andy share valuable insight with each couple, but they are really the words the couple are hearing. The love and respect they have for each other is being communicated. The sensitivity they show each couple is their dialogue. They represent the community. Many couples have expressed how surprised and touched they were to see Phyllis and Andy at their wedding. They truly felt like they cared about them. Perhaps the Sacrament of Marriage is a time to tell these young people that the church is there for them when they need it. That the church will always be there for them. The marriage preparation is a picture, a glimpse of the loving family who waits eagerly for them to return with their own families, to help them fulfill the covenant of their vows to each other and the promise that they made those vows with Jesus as the foundation of their love.

Phyllis and Andy renewed their vows during our 10:00 liturgy. They stood before their three beautiful children, before their church family, before God to celebrate their 25th wedding anniversary. Two people declaring their love for each other and how that love has grown and blossomed in Jesus. Faces that radiated a love that has been tested and refined in the fire. And in the renewal of their covenant was their gift to all young couples, the gift of believing that forever is still true.

Bible

"Your word is a lamp to my feet and a light for my path."
                                          Psalm 119:105

The three wise men traveled in single file on the right side of the sanctuary. They mysteriously made their appearance together and slowly made their way to the manger. So, as a child, it seemed like it had always been that way, three friends starting out on a journey to find the Child Jesus.

It was interesting to ponder in later years how each of the wise men had seen the star from his own home. They left on their journey in hopes of finding the new King. Imagine the night when their caravans merged along the road. Three Kings all from far-off lands. Now they camped together under the stars, enriching their own knowledge through the shared experiences of the group. They talked about what had brought them on this journey. And they decided that from that point, they would like to continue on together.

Each of them possessed a unique gift for the Child. And like all travelers who would find Jesus, we are told that they returned home another way. What a divinely-symbolic way to say that once you find the Lord in your life, you can never go back to things the way they were.

Fifteen years ago, a Bible sharing was started on Sunday morning, one hour before the 10:00 liturgy. People willing to leave their homes in search of finding Jesus. It has been a steady, but small, core group who has faithfully come all that time. We read Scripture, and Father brings in all the new Bible scholarship. Then we share how the reading is our own story. The families in the group learned how to read and enjoy the Bible. The more we understood the background, the culture and the symbols of the Bible, the closer we could come to understanding the true message of Jesus' words to us.

As time went on, interest in the Bible has grown. Families want their children to have a solid base when it comes to Scripture. They wanted to participate in the Sunday morning Bible, yet they were hesitant to join a group that had been journeying together for 15 years. There is something uncomfortable about joining any group, never mind one that has been studying together. Many people felt embarrassed because they didn't know anything about the Bible. What we really needed was to find a nonthreatening way to bring Bible into our community. In our search, we found Serendipity.

Originally, serendipity meant "the facility of making happy chance discoveries" (Horace Walpole, 1743). Applied to Bible study, serendipity is what happens when a group of people get together to share their lives around the Scripture and the Holy Spirit does something special. Because Serendipity is not specifically a Bible Study, we present it in a way we can come together as community, using the Bible as a base. People are assured they do not need any kind of Bible background to join. In a sense, it is like meeting each other at the crossroads. We come like the wise men, all arriving from a different way, all with our information on the Christ Child. But from that point on we want to continue our journey together.

The course is designed for Bible study and nurture, group building and support, and mission and task. It is divided into six-week study sessions that deal with specific themes like success, transition, singles, family, etc. These books offer a good foothold to draw people into the Bible in a comfortable way they can handle. People are personally invited to join a group. By offering a six-week session, most people feel they can make that commitment.

The beauty of the groups is that each one grows according to its own needs. Some groups need more support than Bible. Yet other groups immediately begin serious Scripture study, leaving the smaller series and going right on to the Bible. Each session centers on a Gospel reading. For example, The Storm, Mark 4:35-41. There are open questions to start off the group sharing. Dig questions to read and explore in the text. And reflect questions to take personal inventory on your life. Serendipity raises questions. We use our own study courses and guides to answer specific questions that might arise concerning church teaching and Bible scholarship.

Serendipity is an Upper Room experience. It is an intimate atmosphere where believers can gather to share Jesus in Scripture and bring Him into their own lives. It brings us together to share our own stories of our search for the King. And when we do come together, we begin a serendipitous experience, many happy chance discoveries bringing us closer to finding the hidden secrets of the Kingdom.

We worship together as community, but we need the Upper Room to experience church on a more personal level. To meet quietly, as did the disciples, giving each other strength and sharing the miracles and wonder that Jesus has brought into our lives. We read the Bible passages at home before we come together, and never cease to be amazed how differently the Scripture is revealed when we gather together in His Name. Indeed, when we gather two or more, the Holy Spirit truly enlightens us to the Word, and The Word becomes flesh among us. We have felt the awe of Jesus present because we were willing to leave our homes in search of finding Him.

Serendipity brings the Bible to a personal level. We are put in the story and there we seek to find the "gifts" we possess to give to the King. This type of Bible experience directly helps people to find their ministry in the church. We have many groups meeting at different times of the day and evening. Ideally, we would like to see every member of our church be part of one of the groups. It is hopeful to experience the goodness, the joy, the absolute love people have for the Lord, and their willingness to return that love.

Churches are full of boundless energy just waiting to be tapped into. The Bible is a tool to convert this stored energy into active ministry for the church, as people begin to ask themselves, "What plan does Jesus have for my life?" As they step forward with their "gifts," Father Connolly releases this newfound energy into the community by empowering us to return our talents to Jesus.

We need the upper room experience of small groups to bring us to know one other personally and share Jesus personally. This is what strengthens our church as a whole. It has also led to a greater thirst for the Bible. After being part of the Serendipity groups, many people felt comfortable enough to join the

Sunday morning Bible, and they decided to bring their children. Father announced that he would start the Gospels from the beginning. Indeed, it began a whole new experience.

The Bible is a walk with Jesus, a constant journey where He speaks to us through Scripture. The passage might sometimes be the same, but the conversation is always different. Perhaps the difference comes from the very companions with whom you are walking. They ask Jesus things you never would have thought to ask. As He leads them on their road, you suddenly see whole new horizons opening up before you. "Your Word is a lamp to my feet and a light for my path."

Summer Vacation Bible

The truth is, we began Summer Vacation Bible at our church three years ago, because many of our young people wanted to go and were attending a Bible week at a different church in the area. There was no vacation Bible school offered at any of the Catholic churches in our vicinity. While we were glad they had a place to attend and learn Bible, we try be aware of the expressed needs of our people and look to fulfill those needs through programs within our own community.

The first year we ran a Bible week, word spread like brush fire, and many people called. Invariably, before they hung up they would ask, are you sure this is a Catholic church? We meet with this same surprise over and over again anytime we tell new people that we have Bible studies on Sunday morning, during the week and evenings. Bible is the only book used for Confirmation. And yes, we do have Summer Vacation Bible and yes, we are a Catholic church. The repeated asking of that question was like being given an answer and then having to come up with the question. The answer was Bible. The question was, What do a growing number of Catholics want from the church but don't expect to find?

Summer Vacation Bible is a tremendous success and one of the children's favorite weeks of the year. If it were up to them, they would come for a month. Last year 110 children came to church every day for a week to learn about the great people of the Bible. Each evening, homes were filled with these rich Bible stories and Jesus was present to families in an extra special way.

As one mother came in to pick up her four-year-old, he anxiously ran to her. His blue eyes were twinkling, and he held out his Bible story simply told in a piece of styrofoam that held 10 plastic spoon people, nine of which were dressed in blue and one wearing brown.

To his delight, his mother immediately asked the question he was waiting for. "Why is that one dressed different?"

He proudly told the whole story and ended pointing to the one brown spoon saying, "He was the only one of the 10 lepers who came back to say 'Thank You' to Jesus."

The "Bible story" still sits on his bureau.

Vacation Bible School is scheduled for sometime in July. This is the third year we've offered it. It is for three-year-olds to eighth grade.

The week is a coming together of all the rich resources of our community. The DRE, Pastoral Minister and Youth Minister coordinate the program. But the week involves the work of many men and women who volunteer to teach the classes, and the youth of our parish who are invaluable. The young people are in charge of setting up the snacks, running the games that are held on Wednesday, and doing the necessary footwork that is required all week long.

We have classes Monday and Tuesday. Wednesday, we celebrate liturgy, practicing our procession to repeat on that Sunday for the entire community. Father always gives a beautiful, appropriate and unforgettable homily that ties everything together for both the children and the community. After the morning Mass we spend the rest of the day playing games. Thursday and Friday we resume class.

Each day, every class is given a specific verse to memorize, and a craft or project that pertains to the theme that day. Tables are spread everywhere in the sanctuary, and it is fun to watch the church fill up with beautiful masterpieces created by the work of small hands forming their images of Jesus and the stories of the Bible. Every morning we meet together in the church and Brian, our music minister, leads us in song before we disperse to our individual classes. The strength of our community is felt in so many ways as we share our talents to bring the richness of the Kingdom to life.

Last year "Captain Bob" made a life-sized wooden ark to be the focal of our Bible week which was "People of the Bible."

The ark was placed on the center of the sanctuary, and every boy and girl brought in their favorite animal to live in the ark for the week. The classes each had a turn to go up to visit the ark and sing several songs with Brian about Noah.

Vacation Bible School is the beginning of a journey. It is like making a well-worn path through the Bible where young people can travel comfortably in the Scriptures. When they are older, and ready to resume the journey on their own, they will feel quite surprised at how familiar the roads seem and how sure-footed they have become.

Youth Ministry

"Don't let anyone look down upon you because you are young, but set an example for the believers in speech, in life, in love, in faith and in purity."

1 Timothy 4:12

The youth are the church of today. Having a full-time youth minister in the parish tells the young people in the community that they are important in the life of the parish.

A group of mothers who had just dropped off their children for Junior C.Y.O. had the following conversation. "Do you know what goes on at the meetings?" one mother asked. "I can never get a straight answer from my son." "Neither can I," another mother said. "But it doesn't seem like they do too much religion." Each began to express their concern as to what Junior C.Y.O. was supposed to accomplish. "Well," another mother added, "from what I can get out of my daughter, they don't do too much praying, but since she's started going to Junior C.Y.O. I don't have any more arguments from her about coming to church on Sunday." "I find the same thing happening with my daughter," another mother interjected. "I'm not complaining, but I thought they were going there to learn religion."

This question, "What exactly goes on at C.Y.O.?," has come up so often that Rita, our youth minister, was asked to address this issue at one of our adult sessions at our Religious Education Program. This was her response:

"There are a lot of different things that go on at C.Y.O. It is a place where kids can feel a part of the parish. Presently, we have a large group of kids coming and the number seems to grow each year. While we don't urge kids outside of our parish to come, we don't turn anyone away either.

"We offer young people a place where we all believe the same thing. If they believe in the Lord, then they shouldn't have to be embarrassed of their feelings. This is a place where they can talk about themselves and the Lord and do that without anyone else making fun of them. And this is a place where we work real hard on helping all of them. No one is picked on. You can just come and be made to feel comfortable.

"We have six or seven adults involved. We do a lot of things, especially talking. We try to keep C.Y.O. a social event. We do approach certain subjects, like social justice. We have a family we support through our box project. We work on this once a month. We take care of a whole family from Mississippi. In fact, we were the first ones in the parish to begin the box project.

We're very involved with our region, socially, spiritually and athletically. Through C.Y.O., we play softball, volleyball, and basketball. In fact, we have a lot of award-winning teams, which is not important, but nice. C.Y.O. is a place where kids can play sports and it's somewhat competitive, but not on the level of the high school. Every kid just plays, and they all have equal time. We're real careful about the coaches. We have the Lord in it, and that's the message that we try to spread to the kids.

"We have a lock-in once a year. It's called a lock-in because you go inside for 24 hours and you don't come out. This year 46 youths stayed over. It's done as a community builder. We cook a community meal. From eight till midnight we had Karoake. There are a few breaks in-between. We showed a video, followed by a candlelight rap session that led into a paraliturgy. At three o'clock in the morning we played games and watched more videos. We made breakfast and finished at noon.

"We take the kids to a youth hostel once a year. Usually 40 youths attend and our adult leaders come for the whole weekend, which includes staying over for two nights. Community is the key. If you don't have relationships with the kids, you don't get to anything else.

"People always ask, where does the religion come in? Well, I'm running a Bible group with eight kids who are very serious

and interested in reading Scripture. And several of our kids enrolled themselves in our Confirmation program as a result of
their experience in C.Y.O.

"By the way, for any of you who don't know, C.Y.O., which
stands for Catholic Youth Organization, is for ages 14-19, and
Junior C.Y.O. is for 6th, 7th and 8th grades. The Junior C.Y.O.
meets for one hour every Monday evening. C.Y.O. meets every
Wednesday evening with an "out" night the last Wednesday of
the month. I heard some of the kids talking before, and one of
them said, "Well, what do you do in C.Y.O.?" And she answered, "I'm not really sure, but we have a lot of fun."

And that's what C.Y.O. is about. Having fun, making every
child comfortable, and being there to support them and give
them a feeling of self-worth and acceptance. One mother com-
mented to me that she didn't think we did enough religious
things. And in the next breath she was saying that since her
daughter joined C.Y.O., she's anxious to go to church on Sunday.
She actually asked to go to Summer Vacation Bible cause her
friends were going. Suddenly she wants to be at church whenever she can.

"C.Y.O. gives teenagers a place to meet other teenagers who
have Jesus in their life. It tells them it's cool to have church in
your life." Rita smiled. "I guess that's religious enough for me."

Rita and her husband Mike have a special relationship with
the kids. They have worked tirelessly with the young people in
our parish for years. And so have a great supportive team of
other adults. Yet, one of the best decisions our parish made was
to offer Rita a full-time position as youth minister for our parish.
For the most part, the community does not see the programs
Rita runs. But we clearly see the results of her work. The
young people are anchored at church because they feel the community wants them there.

It is not unusual for kids to drop by the rectory from college
or boot camp, looking for Rita. Then you find out that she has
been quietly writing to them, keeping in touch, reaffirming that
if something is wrong they can come back to church for help. If
they do need guidance, they will get the right guidance from
God to make some tough decisions.

Young people are in and out of the rectory all summer.
There are endless things Rita does to build relationships with
the kids. Just one example is the Graduation Liturgy that Rita

plans. She sends a personal invitation to all of the graduates and invites them to celebrate their achievement with the community. The church is decorated for the occasion and all the graduates are welcome to receive a community cross. So many of the young people were touched that the community cared about them.

Our church is filled with young people. Young people who are no longer leaving the church at 18 because they see that there is something there for them during those years before parenthood brings them back. Two young people in their early twenties are trying to begin a young adult group for single people 21 and older. It is no coincidence that they both have come up through our programs and are comfortably assuming a leadership role in the parish. It was really joyful for the community to have watched these children as they grew up, and now to see them stand before the community as young adult leaders. They are not only a good role model to the teenagers, but offer hope to the parents who have children going through the harder stages of church life.

We have many strong youth leaders in our parish. They do peer ministry for our retreat days. They are invaluable for the week of Vacation Bible School. Many teach a class in our family religious education program. They head Search teams for our region. They represent our parish in many good works outside the church as well. They are leaders in countless other ways, not the least of which is bringing Jesus into school, and into the world around them. They sprinkle our church with their joy, their energy, and their constant search for truth and honesty in religion.

Rita came on staff as our youth minister. Since then she has taken on the enormous responsibility of running our Loaves and Fishes Pantry, a role that requires a lot of energy and time. But no matter how her time is divided, she has eyes for our young people. No matter what the situation, she always sees things in terms of the kids. Through her eyes the kids see the love of a community. Through that love the community sees the youth as the church of today. Youth ministry is relationship.

Mrs. Pizzi

You couldn't have a rainbow without rain.

You couldn't build a house without nails.

You could't sew a quilt without thread.

You couldn't have a door without hinges.

You couldn't have a book without words.

You couldn't have a leader without a follower.

You couldn't have a church without parishioners.

And you definitely couldn't have such a great CYO without all of these excellent members.

But everybody makes mistakes and falls at times and at these times we need somebody to pick us up.

Who is this person, you may be wondering, who is always there for every single member of our CYO?

This person acts just like the nail that keeps the house together. Without her we'd definitely all fall apart.

We all appreciate you even when we don't act it. Thanks for everything and we all love you Mrs. Pizzi.

"St. Blaise Family Banquet, 1993"

Sacrificial Giving

"Bring the whole tithe into the storehouse, That there may be food in my house, and try me in this, says the Lord of hosts: Shall I not open for you the floodgates of heaven, to pour down blessings upon you without measure?"

Malachi 3:10

The two of them sat quietly in the third bench on Sunday morning, a mother and her five-year-old son. The little boy was very curious about everything, especially when he saw men coming down the aisle carrying baskets with long handles. His mother frantically opened her pocketbook. She handed him a quarter.

"Put this in the basket," she said. "Why?" he asked. "This is for Jesus," his mother replied. Just then the basket was passed in front of them. The little boy obediently dropped in his quarter. At the same time he turned to his mother. Perhaps he forgot where he was for the moment, for he asked in a loud voice, "Why does Jesus need money?"

It is fair to say that most churches, including ours, begin sacrificial giving because of financial reasons. In 1984 we had 60 families using envelopes on a weekly basis. Out of the 700 families in the town register who list themselves as Catholic, 350 families were fully active at the time. Our collection ranged between $450.00 and $700.00 for any given weekend. It was at that time we heard of a new parish stewardship program that was working in many churches: Father Joseph Champlin's Sacrificial Giving Program. The program was designed to increase contributions through an awareness of stewardship. After overcoming considerable misgivings, we decided to invite some people in just to explain the program to us.

At their suggestion, the leaders of our community were personally invited to attend the first meeting. The meeting was purposely set up to be as informal as possible. Kitchen chairs were randomly placed around the large dining room. Coffee cups and pastry made a friendly gesture, but were not enough to soften the formality that surrounds any direct discussion of giving habits. Father stood quietly against the wall as the speakers were introduced and began to explain an entirely new concept of giving called sacrificial giving.

"Give back to the Lord a share of what God has given to you," they said. "Make that return a sacrifice. Use church envelopes regularly as gift wrappers for the sacrificial gift. Consider the biblical norm of tithing, 10% of gross income, when determining the actual amount of one's gift. That tithe is normally broken down into five percent for the parish and five percent for the world's poor. Tuition for Catholic schools usually fits into this second five percent."

A new concept of giving was emerging from their presentation. A concept that called us to connect our lives to God through a weekly tithe. An idea that went beyond giving to a cause, whether it be paying the heating bill, replacing a leaky roof, etc.

When they finished, there was a stillness as if all thoughts were being absorbed into the thick carpet beneath us. Faces reflected deep conversations taking place within. Calculations of 10% of gross income. Justification of current weekly giving. Penetration of the truth we had just heard.

"If we give that kind of amount, then we need to know how this money will be used," someone said, finally breaking the silence. The speakers did not seem surprised at the heated discussion that ensued. Father watched his people intently as he listened to the voices rising in the room. "What would the accountability be?" many wanted to know. "Is our parish in debt now? Is that the reason for this program?" a man asked with concern. On and on the discussion continued in a circle that kept leading us back to the beginning. Finally, one woman in the group stood up. In the straightforward, no-nonsense, honest way that was so beautifully characteristic of her, she said, "Either we believe in it or we don't. Correct me if I'm wrong," she continued, "but that's exactly the point I thought was being made. We're not giving to a cause." She raised her hands in the air. "So, why are we asking where the money is going? I'm not saying there should be no accountability. But what I think we have to decide on tonight is if tithing is our responsibility as Christians or not?" she challenged.

That brought an abrupt halt to the discussion. And after everyone got over the initial shock, we agreed that we all needed to take a serious look at our attitudes on giving. With that, the speakers reassured us that no one began by giving 10% of their income. The important thing was to decide on a weekly commitment that represented a sacrifice to your family. Stay with that commitment, and each year try to increase it. The meeting ended.

It was voted that we present the sacrificial giving program to the entire parish. Father was both pleased and relieved with the results of the meeting. The week following the presentation, our collection doubled. And for the next two years the giving remained pretty much the same.

In 1986 we gathered for a finance committee meeting that would sow seeds of new life and, in time, reap a harvest that went far beyond our own planning. It had been two years since we implemented sacrificial giving, and many things that had been talked about during the presentation had not been carried out as of yet. For example, the sacrificial giving guide had suggested we take a look at our envelopes and try to make them more appealing, more representative of the gift we were giving. The program mentioned dropping any second collections that were not mandated by the archdiocese. Was anyone looking into these things?

Someone at the meeting asked if the church had begun to tithe 10% of our income to the poor. Many people had misunderstood about the tithe and had assumed that if we, as parishioners, were expected to give back 10%, then in turn, the church would be responsible for doing the same. "Had this phase of the sacrificial giving program been implemented?" they wanted to know.

For two years families had been sacrificing weekly. Many times they wrote their check to the Lord first, before their own bills were paid. We felt an incredible bond between us that comes from working and sacrificing side by side in the family. People did not want accountability. They truly didn't care about finances. What they were hungering for was knowing their sacrifice was making a difference in the lives of the poor. We, as church, began to feel an overwhelming need to respond to their great love. How could we encourage them? How could we share the good news that we were living the Gospel message of caring for the poor?

Perhaps we needed a tithing committee to tend to this ministry of how we, as church, care for "the orphan, the widow and the stranger among us." The envelopes could be our communication, the eyes for our families to see what their sacrifice meant. Yes, there was much to continue with the sacrificial giving program we had begun.

Without understanding all of the implications at the time, that night was the beginning of a long journey that would lead us to see that tithing is a spiritual, not financial, need for the modern church. Many years later, in our parish report, the bishop would be quite surprised to see that our collections were not listed under finances, but under spiritual growth.

Before the night was over, someone suggested that the parish begin to tithe out of the collection. Everyone was in agreement. Father, as always, completely supported any decision to care for the poor. He took it even one step further. "We should tithe not only from the collection," he said, "but from every dollar that comes through our doors, including bingo." If we were asking families to write their check first to the Lord before all their bills were paid, then we, as church, had to take that same leap in faith.

Two people also volunteered to look into our envelopes. "For General Parish Development" did not exactly reflect the spirit of this return "gift" we were making to the Lord. If caring for the poor was indeed the heart of the Gospel message, and the heart of our church family, we had to be willing to direct new energy and bring new life to our envelope program.

Slowly we found our way. When the envelope companies could not meet our needs, we decided to do the envelopes ourselves. This decision was not made without a real struggle, many questions, and much apprehension. In the end, after much prayer, we decided to go ahead with the project and like everything else we did, we would rely on God to guide us on this completely new road.

An artist in the parish would design each new envelope. We removed the "money boxes" which offended many people. In its place were quotes from Scripture. We brought the finished "envelope" to a small print shop which prints the envelopes exactly as we wish. We have a choice of different-colored inks, and even have a choice of different-colored envelopes. We are excited about our envelopes. People actually began to look forward to seeing what the next envelope would be like. How can the people become excited unless Church is? Yes, it means having to do the mailing ourselves. But this too gives us more control. Because there are no names and dates on the envelopes, we are able to keep envelopes at the entrances of church, which allows new families to sign up when they feel ready. The envelopes are appropriately placed in an old-fashioned brown wooden scoop that is used for grain. A carpenter from our church lovingly made them for us. The envelopes have become OURS. The people sense this. So, with each new step we took, we anxiously shared it with the community.

The very first envelope we designed was a plain white envelope with a big gift-wrap bow in the corner. In the middle of the envelope, written in cursive was: "Our return gift to the Lord." Below simply said "From:_____." Each family wrote their name on the line. The following letter of explanation was mailed with the envelopes.

To Our St. Blaise Family,

> We mail our bills in an envelope. It serves the purpose, meets our obligations. But we wrap our gifts to one another in pretty paper, paper not concerned with

dates or amounts, knowing only the feeling of the gift it holds inside.

Sacrificial giving has made us so aware that our tithe, what we set aside first for the Lord, is our return gift to Him. That is the reason for the new gift wrap.

Many times a year the gift-wrap will change: to reflect the seasons, new feelings that we share as family, to bring excitement and new life to our gifts. Also included with the envelopes will be letters letting you see where we have found the Lord. We are sure you have heard the wonderful news that we, as church, will be giving 10% of all our income to the poor. Thus, we ask that you make us aware of where you have seen the Lord hungry or thirsty. We want the entire community to share in this decision.

The gift-wrap, the new envelopes, is to be the communication for our St. Blaise family. Write on the back of your envelope or enclose a note inside. We must find the Lord together.

We hope the new gift-wrap and letters will bring joy to your life, something you will look forward to receiving. Perhaps the greatest joy in the world comes from feeling your life can make a difference.

Yours in the family,

Out of the entire community, there was only one negative response. The rest of the people responded wholeheartedly. Though our collections had doubled with sacrificial giving, people still reacted poorly to using envelopes. Now 60 families jumped to 120 in a matter of weeks. And we received two letters in the envelopes suggesting places where we could help the poor.

The first place was in our area, a soup kitchen called Because He Lives. It had just recently opened. Two members in our community visited Paul Dempster, who was in charge of the kitchen, and listened to his plan for helping the poor. He was not just interested in feeding them, but wanted to know why they needed to be fed. What could be done to make them self-sufficient? We knew this was the kind of place our community could make a difference in empowering the poor. The second suggestion was a mission in Appalachia, in Harlan, Kentucky. We wrote to them and established a personal contact.

All of this was conveyed to the community through the envelopes. And the more people heard about our work with the poor, the more our collections began to rise. In the beginning, people were giving half of their tithe to church for church support, and with the other half they were on their own to care for the poor. Yet the more involved we became with tithing, a clear picture of the early Church revealed itself to us. The people in the early Church brought their whole tithe to the temple and THE CHURCH was the channel to care for the poor among them. Biblical tithing—THIS WAS THE MISSING LINK. Jesus instituted the Church to care for the poor. He never intended individual families to take on that responsibility.

Now this made sense. We, as church, taking care of the poor through The Body of Christ, the people. Families desperately wanted to feed the hungry and clothe the naked, to live the Gospel message Father so clearly spelled out. But for the most part, they felt insignificant and did not know how to go about it. Many were disheartened by the exposing of frauds when it came to the poor. They did not have the means or the time in many cases to look into organizations. Now, they were being asked through community to suggest ways and places to help the poor. They were asked to vote to continue our tithing every year. But the church assumed the rightful, awesome duty of becoming the channel of distribution and the most careful of stewards for the poor.

We personally looked into every place we gave, visiting the closer ones. We established a direct line of communication with the missions we now had in El Salvador, Appalachia, Ethiopia, and Haiti. Many of the missions began with a personal contact. They wrote back each month, assuring us that they had received "our tithe." The Pastoral Minister became the link between our missions and the community. She was the eyes for the church family to "see" and share the wonder and love that was a direct result of their sacrifice, their weekly return gift to the Lord.

A most important thing was happening. A trust relationship between church and the community was beginning. They trusted the church to be their channel to care for the poor. For most, this was a great relief. Many people dropped notes in their envelopes saying they had stopped giving anywhere else.

They felt their giving one large amount to church could make a greater difference than giving a smaller amount to many places. The power of tithing was happening for us.

Our collections are five times what they were. From 60 families using envelopes, we now have 280 out of a parish that has grown to 450 active families. Most of our families make a weekly commitment. But it is never numbers that impress us. It is the awareness of the great changes that have happened to us ever so gently, so gradually, changes recognized more clearly in retrospect.

A few weeks ago, Mass was canceled due to a blizzard. The following week, our collection was double almost to the penny. That would never have happened several years ago: people connecting their lives to God through tithing every week, not the weeks they go to church.

Success is knowing that we have reached a point where we feel our envelopes indeed reflect our return gift to the Lord. Knowing that we have reached our people. We now understand that tithing cannot be understood in terms of what people give. Tithing must be perceived in terms of the whole picture. People giving in order that the church may fulfill her responsibility of caring for the "widow, the orphan and the foreigner," the Biblical symbols for the poor.

Beyond Envelopes

Sacrificial giving must be kept alive and brought into the community through other visible means besides the envelopes themselves. My husband and I gave a sacrificial giving presentation to a nearby parish. We spoke to many in the community after the Mass. None of them knew how their church was involved with helping the poor. Yet, their pastor was on the board of directors for a local food kitchen. Their church did much to help the poor. While the bulletin posted the weekly collections and made a financial report, there was no reporting on the good news of caring for the poor.

Each church has its own network of programs, including the bulletin, that can be used as channels of information for the community. Once a church begins sacrificial giving, it is important to keep it alive in the whole community, not just to those in

the envelope program. One way is to give tithing presentations during the year. We give two tithing presentations, one in the fall, and one in the spring. Both are given on religious education Sundays when we can be assured of having the best representation of our parish in attendance. The presentations are given during the homily at all the Masses. This is especially important for the new families who are constantly joining our church and are not familiar with sacrificial giving. And it is important to constantly reinforce what we already know about tithing. The bulletin and the adult session of our religious education program are valuable tools to educate people further on tithing itself and how we as church are outreaching to the poor. One religious education program was devoted specifically to parish outreach. The DRE began the program with a powerful presentation on the difference between charity and social justice. She explained the Box Project that the 4th, 5th and 6th grades were involved with through their classes. The Box Project is an inexpensive way to connect to a poorer family through mailing items on hand, like bars of soap, clothing, etc. The children correspond directly with the family and learn first-hand how people in poorer sections of our country live. Once a month, the class does a mailing. It is a real eye-opener for our kids.

The Pastoral Minister spoke of the sacrificial giving program, who we give to, how decisions are reached, and how this has affected the poor. The youth minister, who also handles our food pantry, gave an overview of the pantry, when it began, the people coming, etc. MaryAnn, the contact person for Ethiopia, shared some interesting insight on our mission there.

The children in some of the grades were involved in making "soup can" banks for the food pantry. All the classes were involved with the poor.

That Sunday the theme of sacrificial giving was carefully created throughout the community. It began with a beautiful homily and was carried through the liturgy by the music people. New envelopes were mailed out the week of religious education, a white envelope with a rich brown ink. The Scripture on the envelope was from John 12:24: "A grain of wheat remains no more than a single grain unless it is dropped into the ground and dies. If it does die, then it produces many grains." The artwork was three stalks of wheat and a loaf of bread. The stalks of wheat represented individual families. The bread was the result of what we could become when we "died" to ourselves and sacrificed for the Lord. The bulletin featured the same artwork as the envelopes and invited new people in the community to join in the envelope program.

Our outreach to the poor must become visible and part of our celebrations. There are many ways of turning abstract giving into moments of seeing the reason and plan for our return gift.

One year in November, Gerry, our religious education director, invited Paul Dempster to be our guest speaker for the adult session. As was previously mentioned, Paul heads the food kitchen that we tithe to on a monthly basis. The people in our community knew about Because He Lives, the name of the food kitchen, and had often heard Paul's name. Now he stood before them. In a soft-spoken voice, he painted pictures of the people who came to the kitchen. He told of an elderly woman in her 70s who came in and literally fell down the ramp. Appearing drunk, they soon discovered she was diabetic and had to choose between food and her medicine. He explained that because he could count on our monthly tithe, he had been able to set up a prescription fund for the elderly.

This humble, slender man, with the presence of the Spirit about him, spoke of the dignity of the working poor. We learned of an English class that was offered to the many foreigners in the area and of a class on citizenship. How employment and housing was being found for many. They were finding out why people were hungry. Our eyes were opened to much we didn't know existed right on our doorstep.

He closed with this story. "One night in the early days of our opening the kitchen, my wife Pat and I were sitting at one of the tables. We looked around at all that had been accomplished already. We had just made a list of all of our bills and had written the amount down on a piece of paper. My wife looked at me and said, "I don't know what we're going to do. There's no money left to pay this." I threw my hands up in the air and said, "Jesus you led us here. You called us to do this ministry, and if you want these doors to stay open, then you have to take care of it."

He paused and a remembering smile radiated on his face. "Not two minutes later," he continued to say, "two people from your community came walking down the ramp and handed us a check. They explained that their church had decided to make a monthly contribution from their tithing, but to begin with, they wanted to give us a donation that night. Well, I never thought to open it while they were there. We continued to talk and I put it in my pocket. I thought perhaps it was a check for $50.00 or maybe $100.00. And I would have been very grateful to receive that. They left and I only remembered the check later that evening. I took the check out of my pocket, and Pat and I looked at it together. It was a check for $1,000.00. We literally began to cry. We knew you had no way of knowing that, to the penny, that was the amount we had written down on the piece of paper."

Through Paul the Word became flesh and dwelt among us that morning. Jesus came to us as He always did, through the poor. People wept openly. He was using our hands to do His work. We felt united, indeed, the Body of Christ, the church. For many weeks to follow, those envelopes echoed the words and stories Paul shared, and spoke to us, "I was hungry, and you gave me to eat."

Always New

If you walked in our church this Sunday, you would find a table with a huge shimmering punch bowl filled with the most beautiful shiny buttons one could imagine: tiny strawberries, coal black jewels, wispy white buttons as delicate as Queen Ann's lace. Shy buttons and enormous bold ones that reach out to capture your attention.

These buttons speak of us. Our uniqueness, the reality of what we can accomplish together. They are there because our mission in Ethiopia asked if we could send them. They are beginning a sewing project for the women. This project will allow them to earn a small living for their family. MaryAnn made a plea for buttons during the Masses. One little boy was so moved and so excited that his mother had to stop him from ripping the buttons off his shirt right then and there! "They need the buttons more than I do," he protested. After some coaxing, his mother assured him they could find some buttons at home.

Along with the punch bowl, MaryAnn arranged a lovely display. She did a collage with a map showing where Ethiopia is located, along with various touching, personal pictures that they have sent us over the years. All the handwritten letters we have received since 1984 are available for people to read. Near the table is a handmade, cloth-framed picture of a woman grinding meal that the people in Ethiopia made and sent our community as a gesture of gratitude.

The people gather weekly after Mass, watching as the punch bowl spills over to hold an entire box of buttons, including two handmade button strings that were donated and we decided to wear every week in our procession.

Button strings that would rival any gold necklace. Families were so excited and interested to "see" our mission in Ethiopia that we decided to feature a different place we tithe to each month.

Our connections to our brothers and sisters around the world are as simple as the buttons in the glass bowl: buttons that represent the ordinary living of our lives; buttons intended to hold things together. They truly represent our church family: the variety, the colors, and especially the "multiplication" that happens when we come together for the Lord's purpose through the way He intended, the Church. As the children reach in the bowl and let the buttons slip through their fingers, and the parents read the letters, Ethiopia becomes real. New families ask how they can join the envelope program to be part of this touching experience. Questions are raised about our work with the poor. The abstract of giving becomes real in the faces we see before us. And around that table, many people discover "Why Jesus needs money."

Jacob's Ladder

We began sacrificial giving because of financial reasons. What we discovered was that sacrificial giving leads church back to "the ladder," Jacob's ladder. At the foot of the ladder is the gateway, tithing. Each church has a different stairway. The climb has to become your own, taken through your own programs, your own people, your own spirituality.

It is appropriate to end with the last tithing presentation that was given to our community, Jacob's Ladder.

If there was a stairway reaching from earth to heaven, would you want to climb it?

One night, Jacob, the grandson of Abraham and Sarah, had a dream. This is the story of Jacob's dream as recorded in the book of Genesis, the first book of the Bible.

Jacob lay down to sleep, resting his head on a stone. He dreamed that he saw a stairway reaching from earth to heaven, with angels going up and coming down on it. And there was the Lord, the God of Abraham and Sarah, standing beside him. 'Through you and your descendants,' the Lord said, 'I will bless all the nations. Remember, I will be with you and protect you wherever you go.'

Then Jacob woke up and said, 'The Lord is here! He is in this place, and I didn't know it! This must be the gate that opens into heaven.' Jacob got up early the next morning, took the stone that was under his head, and set it up as a memorial. There he made a vow to the Lord. 'If you will be with me and bless me, then you will be my God, and in return, I will give you a tenth of everything you give me.'

It is interesting that the very first thing Jacob did when he recognized God in his life was to establish a tangible way to connect his own life to God's. And he did this by promising to return to the Lord a tenth of all he received.

Can you picture how well this worked? Every time Jacob looked at his growing flocks, he would remember God by thinking, "This part of the flock belongs to me, but this part belongs to God who blesses me."

In everything Jacob owned he began to see God's share. And maybe it was easier in those times to picture God's share when people gave back sheep, bags of grain, and a portion of their harvest. This was the physical reaping of a family's blessings. Don't you agree that it is harder for us, today, to constantly remind ourselves that our return gift, our tithe, represents our family's blessings: our food, our shelter, our clothing? It is difficult for us, for though we are the descendants of Jacob, we have not remembered God through tithing for many generations.

It is time for us to return to Jacob's ladder. And, like Jacob, to connect our lives to God again through tithing. Tithing is mentioned throughout the Bible, beginning with Abraham in Genesis. But Jacob's ladder presents the picture of how tithing happens in our lives. For tithing is indeed like climbing a ladder. We must take one step at a time. It has been suggested that a good way to begin is to start by giving back one hour of our weekly wage. Every week we connect our lives to God in this way. And soon, in everything that comes to us, we will begin to see God's share. Gradually, we try to increase the amount we give as we work our way up the ladder.

A few months ago, an engineer came to our church. Like many other churches, we had to have our underground oil tank removed. We were glad to comply since it was to protect the earth from possible oil spillage. However, we had a 6,000 gallon tank and it was a costly project. The engineer immediately suggested we have a drive to raise the money.

I explained to him we don't believe in drives, we don't give to a cause, we do tithing. He was curious. "You know," he said, "I go all over the archdiocese and I hear mention of sacrificial giving and tithing. What exactly is tithing?" he asked. "Well, tithing is giving back a portion of what you earn—eventually leading up to giving back a tenth of your weekly income." He was measuring something and quickly turned to me and said, "Do you mean to tell me you expect a poor family to give back 10% of their income to church?" I looked directly at him and asked, "Do you expect a wealthy family to?"

You know, it's so human to think it's easier for some to give than others. But the truth is, tithing will be equally hard for each family here. It has little to do with how much you make.

Once you decide to tithe, the first steps are not too difficult. Most families can afford to give one hour of their weekly wage. In fact, there is an instant peace and joy that comes to you when God becomes a tangible part of your life. And you will want to climb many steps on the ladder. But there will come a point when you reach a certain plateau and the only way you can climb higher is by simplifying your life, and changing your lifestyle. Each family knows what they have to do to reach that next step. It will be difficult.

And why shouldn't it be? Since we were children, the world has been holding out its own ladder. A ladder you climb by making more, accumulating more, storing more. And we're told that this will make us happy.

The world's ladder. Jacob's ladder, a stairway from earth to heaven. What will move us to start a journey that begins with tithing, giving something away?

Indeed, many will decide not to. "But, if today, you hear his voice, harden not your hearts. Stir into flame the gift God bestows upon you. With the strength that comes from God bear your share of the hardship which the Gospel entails."

Climb the ladder. Know that it is Jesus who holds THIS ladder. He will not allow you to fall. And when you become afraid, say to the Lord, "Increase my faith." And He will tell you, "If you had faith the size of a mustard seed, you could say to the sycamore, be uprooted and it would obey you." We are the sycamore, so rooted to the earth, so afraid to let go and allow Jesus to take us to new heights. Let go—Climb!

At first, you won't notice how high you've climbed, or that climbing the ladder has changed your life. But it will be revealed to you, if only in small ways in the beginning. You'll be standing in line at the checkout one day, and the people in line with you will be looking at their watches, complaining how they've been waiting for five minutes. And instead of being one of the aggravated, you find yourself quite at peace thinking of one of our tithing families in Haiti who walked four days for a portion of rice.

Slowly, through tithing, you are given a different view of the world, one they cannot see. You're looking at the world from this new height. Suddenly the words have true meaning: "The Lord is here. He is in this place and I didn't even know it." The Lord is standing beside me. Everywhere you look you see God. You have found the gate, the tangible way to connect your life to God's through tithing.

For indeed, there is a stairway, called Jacob's ladder, which connects earth to heaven. But do you want to climb it?

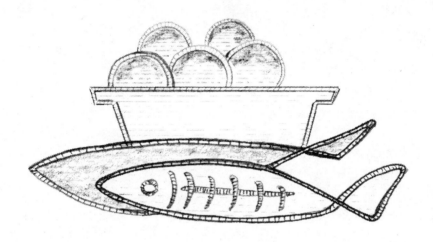

The Loaves and Fishes Food Pantry

"They do not need to go away.
You give them something to eat."

Matthew 14:16

Two thousand years ago, a large crowd began to follow Jesus. They left their villages, and when evening came, the disciples went to Jesus and said, "Send the people away, back to the village where they can get food." But Jesus turned to them and said, "You give them something to eat." That small group of disciples stood among a crowd of 5,000 people (not counting the women and children) with five loaves and two fish in their hands. And simply because Jesus said so, they began to feed the crowd with what they had. Soon, everyone in the crowd began to share what they had. "They all ate and were satisfied, and the disciples picked up twelve baskets of broken pieces that were left over."

That was the idea behind our Loaves and Fishes food pantry. Simply, we would begin to feed "the crowd" with what we had among us. The idea was planted when Paul Dempster, who runs a food kitchen in Woonsocket, spoke at one of our Religious Education Sundays. He told us that he was seeing more and more people from the Bellingham area at the food kitchen. Paul said he thought there would be a great need for a food pantry in Bellingham. The people in the parish responded. Many ideas were presented, and several people offered to help. But in the end, we realized the pantry had to be housed at church and it needed someone who would be there to take complete charge. Rita, who is our youth minister, found herself being called to take on this new ministry.

The Loaves and Fishes Food Pantry opened its doors on January 23, 1991. In January four families were fed. Now we're feeding 40 familes a month, some once a week. As a community we fed 41 families for Thanksgiving and took care of their entire Christmas.

The pantry is confidential. The needs are met in a personal way. Rita knows who drinks coffee or tea, and what formula the baby is on. The families receive a full supply of groceries. They are often surprised at what they find in the bags, and perhaps never expect the friend they find in Rita. When a crisis hits, Rita is the first person they will call. And many of the women have climbed out of bad situations through the support of the community and from Rita's care. Some have come back to share the good news and tell Rita how well they're doing. We are careful not to push religion. Yet, several of the families who came to the pantry have since joined our parish. A few come to playgroup regularly. But we hope that all of them will someday realize that when they were at their lowest, it was the church who fed them. It was the church who cared what happened to them. The children do not fully understand why these bad things are happening to their family. But they are learning that after their parents come home from church, things are always better. Church must indeed be a wonderful place.

The pantry is mostly supported by the people of our community. Each week families bring in their food for the pantry; mothers are often prompted by children who ask, "What are we getting for the pantry this week?" The food is placed on the side of the sanctuary where a basket is always kept. A portion of our tithe is used to purchase food vouchers which enable families to buy milk and meat, items we cannot keep on hand. Proceeds from the Lighthouse Coffeehouse help fund the pantry. And now we have Loaves and Fishes cards that can be given for many occasions. We have other groups, like St. Brendan's, the Scouts, school groups and local businesses who use our church building and who will collect food and paper goods for our pantry or make a donation.

When we opened the doors for the pantry, no one imagined how much food we would be giving out. We began to give what we had and the baskets never emptied. We stopped focusing on how large the crowd was, and turned our eyes on Jesus. Start by giving what you have, He commanded. And as we stepped with faith into the pages of the feeding of the five thousand, we found ourselves right in the middle of the same miracle.

Peace and Justice

"The Spirit of the Lord is upon me, because he has anointed me to preach good news to the poor. He has sent me to proclaim release to the captives and recovering of sight to the blind, to set at liberty those who are oppressed, to proclaim the acceptable year of the Lord."
Isaiah 61:1-2 / Luke 4:18-19

We have all heard the story about a village that had a strong river flowing near it. One day, a body came floating down the river. The villagers fished the body out, saw that the person was still alive, brought it to the hospital, gave it medical care. The next week there were two bodies. Then there were more and more bodies floating down the river and they continued taking care of them. Finally, someone in the village said, "Why don't we go up river and find out why the bodies are coming down? And perhaps we can do something about the problem."

As community we try to "go up river." For the most part Father Connolly and Gerry, our DRE, help us in our journey. Gerry heads the Urgent Action Network of Amnesty International for our parish. This network calls upon its participants to send letters and telegrams to government officials in response to persons who are in extreme danger, e.g., the victims of abduction, unacknowledged detention, torture, or other life-threatening situations. Participation is straightforward and does not demand much time. Usually an hour or two set aside on a monthly basis is sufficient to discuss a case and write letters/telegrams on behalf of specific prisoners. Gerry meets after Mass with all parishioners who are interested in this letter-writing ministry. She keeps the community informed of the release of prisoners that happens as a direct result of this letter-writing.

Gerry is a brilliant woman who keeps well informed on issues of social justice. Faithfully, she reads alternative publications that share political truth. She plans most of our liturgies that revolve around social justice, and has a true feel for using visible signs to put people in touch with their feelings. One example is the December celebration of the Martyrs in El Salvador.

In this case she incorporates the pictures we have hanging in our church throughout the year as the visible signs. The community is asked to remain seated during the procession that begins after Gerry's brief explanation. "Today is the second Sunday of Advent. Advent is the time Christians prepare for the coming of Jesus. A time for us to think about and act on how Jesus is calling us to peace in our world. We Christians, that is, believers and followers of Jesus, hold a belief that there is a future for human beings. Jesus gives meaning to our lives. Today in our entrance procession, we will be recognizing a few who because of their beliefs, and acting on those beliefs, have given special meaning to their lives."

The church is solemn and prayerful as the procession makes its way down the aisle, with Gerry's voice setting the rhythm:

First, we have the Cross.

Next is the Book of the Word of God.

The Book of the Word of God for the Children's Liturgy.

Pictures of our martyrs of El Salvador: Sr. Ita Ford, Sr. Dorothy Kazel, Sr. Maura Clark and Jean Donovan; December 2, 1992 was the 12th Anniversary of their martyrdom.

A picture of the Jesuit priests who were martyred November 16, 1989.

A picture of Dorothy Day, Martin Luther King Jr., and Gandhi.

A picture of Mary, Mother of the Missing from Argentina.

Our wall hangings from Ethiopia and Haiti that were a gift to us from the missions we tithe to.

We are also carrying in our hearts the Sisters murdered in Liberia this year. Also, all those suffering starvation in Somalia and Bosnia. Father is carrying in a picture of Archbishop Romero. Romero knew that his stand with the poor would put his life at risk. He said, "If they kill me—I shall arise in the Salvadoran people. Let my blood be a seed of freedom, and a sign that hope will soon be a reality."

What all have in common is that each person was working to help empower the powerless. The problems in the world today have to do with power, not power itself, but the abuse of power. For our readings today, Gerry and Leoné will read. Leoné is from South Africa, a country that is often in the news because of the abuse of power.

How simply and effectively the tone was set for liturgy—the Word of God coming directly from the powerless!

Gerry brings the parish to an awareness of peace through many visible signs throughout the year. This year, for "Peace Pentecost," she asked that families write a peace petition just for themselves, the letters were not going to be read by anyone. When the table was being set, families were asked to bring up their petitions as part of our prayer and to place them in a basket that was on the altar.

Our August bulletin celebrates Peace Day. The first Monday in August we have a prayerful outdoor liturgy in remembrance of the atrocity of the nuclear devastation that killed over 200,000 people in the bombings of Hiroshima and Nagasaki.

Each time we celebrate peace as community, the message of peace is brought into the home. One of the planned topics for religious education this winter is peace. How are we teaching our children to solve their problems? Church must be a channel of peace in our violent society.

Since the early 70s Father has encouraged the people of the parish to write letters to our state and local representatives, and to the president, to voice our feelings against war or any action that is taken by our government that violates human rights.

The first Monday of each month is our Peace Vigil, where members of the community meet in the center of town to pray for peace. During the Gulf War, Father invited members from NISBCO (National Interreligious Service Board for Conscientious Objectors) to speak to the community about what it means to be a Conscientious Objector. He has informative literature available for the community, like Ronald Musto's book, *The Catholic Peace Tradition*, and various leaflets from CCCO (Central Committee for Conscientious Objectors). It is eye-opening to see the pacifist church that existed for the early Christians when the wood was green, the first 300 years of the church when Christians were not allowed to join the military. As Albert Nolan so perfectly puts it, "Jesus Before Christianity," before the church took on the politics of the Roman Empire in the 4th century.

Yet, perhaps the most powerful way we bring peace into our community is through Father himself. Every Sunday Father walks down the center aisle to ask the people for their prayers of petition. When everyone has given their requests, he slowly backs up the middle of the aisle and stops. He lifts his arms out and says his own prayer of petition that every single person in the church, to the youngest of the children, can repeat word for word:

> God created this little planet earth for his children to live on for a short while. And being a loving Father, He put enough resources for every child of His to live a full human life. But for those in power in our world who take these resources and turn them into instruments of war, or use them for greed, then we pray against these, and pray for an economy of peace. Lord hear our prayer.

"Lord hear our prayer," the community responds. And perhaps that is the answer. We hear the sounds of peace in our churches until we can echo them and reproduce them in the world.

The Lighthouse

*"Bring my sons from afar and my daughters from the
ends of the earth."*

Isaiah 43:6

On top of the flat roof that protectively extends itself over the
doors of the entrance of our church sits a small lighthouse. It was
built to remind people to come to the Lighthouse Coffee House
that is held the third Saturday of each month at 7:30 p.m. in the
basement of our church.

The coffee house features checkered tablecloths, candlelight
and a beautiful sound system. There is a suggested donation
which benefits the Loaves and Fishes Food Pantry that St. Blaise
sponsors. Home-baked pastries and gourmet coffee is served.

The Lighthouse Coffeehouse began with one small light, the
light of two professional musicians, Brian and Cindy, who offered their talents as liturgical singers at the Sunday liturgy.
Their gifts were so enlightening and powerful that the community asked if they would present an entire evening of music that
would be open to all. That two-hour presentation was the beginning of The Lighthouse Coffeehouse, which provides a peaceful, intimate atmosphere where believers can come together and
share the message of Jesus through the power of song. For
many, The Lighthouse has become a night to slow down the fast
pace of life and to rekindle the light of Jesus. Even the best
lights need tending and the Lighthouse is just the place for that.

In December, one might find the magic of the Christmas
story. Or in April, a walk on the Via Dolorosa. You never know.
One might even stumble on a miracle, if you believe in such
things.

Duke is a regular at the coffeehouse, at least on those nights
when he can make it out. He suffers from MS and is confined

to a wheelchair. One day Brian heard a song that was just for
Duke. Many times Brian will sing a song at the coffeehouse
with a particular audience member in mind, never knowing if
that person will come that night or not. That whole night was
geared to singing that song for Duke. The song, titled "This
Thorn," was about pain, the fellowship of pain with Jesus.

It was planned for the second half of the evening. At the
end of the first set, Duke became ill and decided to leave. He
got into the handicapped elevator and pressed "up." He went
up a few feet and the elevator came right back down. This happened twice.

Duke read this as a sign that for some reason he was meant
to stay for the second half of the evening. Once he had made
the decision, the elevator, which is only a year old, worked perfectly. It took him upstairs to inform his wife that they were
staying. He went back down and listened to the second set. At
no time did Brian mention to Duke or anyone that he was going
to sing a song for him.

When Brian left for the night he noticed a note on the wind-
shield of his car. The note read, "Thank you for 'This Thorn.'
Duke." Brian would not find out till days later what had actually happened.

Skeptics would say the elevator malfunctioned. Others
would simply chalk it up as coincidence. But then, that's how it
is with the Light: you never know who will see it.

The long-term goal of the coffeehouse is to keep it going. It
is ever-new and ever-changing. Brian and Phyllis now run the
coffeehouse and are the featured "house" performers, doing the
first hour each month. The hour is a combination of stories and
songs that are Scripture-based and carefully woven around a
theme. Their ministry at the Lighthouse Coffeehouse has led to
many guest appearances around New England, where they have
been invited to share "The Lighthouse" (which they have
adopted as the name of their ministry), to groups that vary from
religious educators to youth groups to community.

The coffeehouse now incorporates guest performers from the
area, who perform the second half of the evening. It is ecumeni-
cal and provides a wonderful window to see Jesus from different
views. It is exciting to watch the Lighthouse take different
shapes as Jesus creates from the "lanterns" we hold.

In the beginning, Brian thought of many names for the coffeehouse. But when The Lighthouse seemed to pop out of thin air, he was absolutely certain that was to be its name. He wasn't sure exactly why. Like everything God does in your life, the reasons were slowly revealed. As Brian studied lighthouses, he realized that in a very symbolic way Jesus is the Lighthouse. He is the keeper of the light guiding us safely home. Brian has written many songs that speak of this theme.

The lights are in constant danger. There are a growing number of good people who are drumming up awareness to conserve and protect the lights. In 1915 America had 4,499 lights and some 29,243 people caring for the towers. But, one by one, the keepers are gone and slowly the lights are being extinguished. In a real sense, we too, are part of God's plan to rekindle the lights in a world where they are slowly being extinguished.

In our study of lighthouses, we found that each lighthouse is unique. Some are wooden, some brick, others iron or granite. Each has been designed and given a particular coded light that no other lighthouse has. As we come to know The Light, we too must be a light for others.

On the top of our church sits a small lighthouse. It was built to be a reminder of the Lighthouse Coffeehouse. Yet, we have come to see a much greater purpose for the little lighthouse.

You see, there are so many people who are in danger of crashing. Yet, they are so close to home. At dusk, a warm yellow light blinks into the darkness. It's right there for everyone who takes time to look for it. The light sends out a continuous signal that says, "Bring my sons from afar and my daughters from the ends of the earth." Come, this is the way home . . .

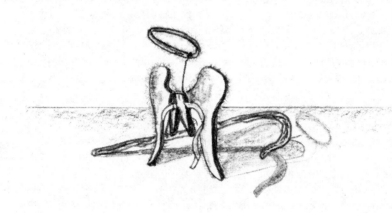

Family

*'Well done, good and faithful servant! You have been
faithful with a few things; I will put you in charge of
many things; Come and share your Master's happiness!'*
                                                    Matthew 25:21

Traditions

Back in St. Patrick School in Natick, when I was young, we
had a Christmas Eve tradition. All the children in grades four
through nine would stand around the outdoor manger scene and
sing Christmas carols. People of the parish would stand on the
sidewalk or sit in their cars to listen to us. I remember that
Christmas seemed to start then, as we stood crunching the snow
with our buckled overshoes and singing our well-practiced
songs. When we finished, we would crowd into the nearby corner drugstore and drink hot chocolate with whipped cream on
top and two saltine crackers tucked into the saucer. We would
feel warm and Christmasy as we hummed snatches of the carols
we had just finished singing.

The next morning we, of course, would go to Christmas
Mass, but there we were only observers, so I have little memory
at those services. I can still feel the carol sing, though, because I
was a part of it. It lived for me.

Here at St. Blaise, in the 1990s, we also have Christmas traditions. On Christmas Eve we have a family Mass with special
music, liturgical dance, and a living gospel telling the Christmas
story. A live donkey brings Mary to Bethlehem and the children
of the parish are the shepherds and angels who welcome Jesus.

We will have a practice for this pageant on the Sunday evening before Christmas at 5:00 p.m. It will last about an hour. Children through the sixth grade are invited to be shepherds or angels. We are encouraging you to bring your children to the practice so that they, too, can develop memories of being a part of the Christmas story, memories that will be a part of them forever.

Carolyn, her husband Tom, and their two children Anne and Michael, now in their 20s, are in charge of "traditions" at St. Blaise. They are an artistic, gifted family who bring drama and dance to our community. Each has his/her own unique talent. Carolyn coordinates, writes and directs. Tom is the set up person who runs the lighting. Michael is a photographer who captures the community in touching, poignant slides that Carolyn skillfully weaves at presentations for Penitentials and other services. Michael also does sound and unusual lighting effects. Anne is a choreographer and teaches liturgical dance. She also teaches drama and creates prayer in that medium.

One November during Thanksgiving week, Anne fashioned a meditation that brought the community to tears. From the back of the church, the children wove down the aisle with hands connected like the rope of a chain gang. Each was dressed in a native costume. Their covered heads were hung low and their innocence cut through the heart. They were the refugee children of the world. Through their powerful dance they brought the child refugee into our midst in a way that words cannot express. They brought the community to one mind. They brought their family together, as almost every parent was there to see their child dance, even the ones who do not go to church, yet!

Children's lives revolve around seasons in which they participate. Baseball. Soccer. Volleyball. Carolyn and Anne bring the children into the church seasons. During Lent, most of the children are involved in the Holy Days. On Good Friday we have a multiliturgy presentation of the Stations of the Cross. There is dance, drama, readings and music. Easter Sunday is alive with liturgical dancers bringing new life into the church. All year the children are involved and brought into the different liturgical seasons of the church.

Yet Christmas Eve has a magic all its own. There is standing room only as the donkey carries Mary and Joseph to Bethlehem. The benches are full of angel wings, staffs, and memories.

One mother recalls the first year her son was a shepherd. The voice read aloud, "An angel of the Lord appeared to them, and the glory of the Lord shone over them and they feared exceedingly." And all the little shepherds, whose backs were to the community, made gestures of fear as arms were raised in different positions. All except for her son, who kept still.

"Why didn't you look afraid?" she asked him after the service.

In his most serious voice, he answered, "But Ma, you didn't see my eyes!"

The community watches as young shepherds graduate to wise men. A little angel becomes Mary. The church is warm and Christmasy as the children become a part of the Christmas story.

After the live Gospel is over, the angels and shepherds join their families. One of the young dancers gracefully leaps up onto the sanctuary, holds the baby Jesus high in the air, and prayerfully places the Child in the manger. She speaks for all as she reaches down to pull the small chain that lights the manger. A Light that will live on forever in these beautiful sacred traditions.

Special Needs

"Since the passing of the ADA (Americans with Disabilities Act) this past summer, we have all become more aware of the importance of understanding the special needs of our brothers and sisters with disabilities and life challenges," Jacky announced. Jacky has long been an advocate for this cause and has a master's degree in social work. "We as church community need education and a more specific awareness of those special needs. Our need is also to know what accommodations we can make in order to assist our challenged brothers and sisters.

"It is so important that all of our ministries, activities and celebrations are available and accessible to everyone. We must turn our barriers into bridges!

"In order for this to happen, we are calling all those who are interested in this special ministry, particularly those who have a personal understanding of specific needs, to come forward and share ideas and generate a plan for our community.

"This calling is very special indeed. So, if you have an idea to share or would like to learn more about being an advocate for our community, please come to our meeting next Sunday, following the 10:00 am Mass."

Twenty people came to the first meeting, many of whom are professionals in related fields, including Ann who works with the hearing-impaired and does signing for some of our special liturgies. We opened the meeting by discussing what we do have to offer. We are handicapped-accessible, with wheelchair-accessible rest rooms, and we have an elevator. We have specially-challenged brothers and sisters who are an important part of many of our celebrations, including dance and drama. We have good lighting and an excellent sound system. And we feel people with disabilities can and are encouraged to participate in all of the programs and activities offered by our parish. Where do we go from here?

Five people volunteered to participate in sessions that were offered as part of the Certification Program for Parish Advocates sponsored by the Office for Persons with Disabilities, which is directed by Pat Friel. The primary role of the parish advocate, who serves in a volunteer capacity, is to assist the pastor and parish staff in pastoral care for persons with disabilities and their families. The advocate is an on-site resource person who can coordinate ministry with persons with disabilities and serve as a liaison between the pastor, parish staff, parish ministries, and the Archdiocesan Office. Two people from the parish received their certification and three attended most of the sessions. Other people have signed up for different workshops to be held in the upcoming year.

Ann is in the process of visiting other parishes who have a sign language interpreter. She hopes to begin signing on our religious education Sundays. One of the men in the group is looking into assistive listening devices for those who are hard of hearing. Someone in the group mentioned that the step up to the sanctuary prevents people in wheelchairs from reading or being Eucharistic Ministers. People suggested that a permanent ramp would make more of a welcoming statement. There are plans to have an engineer come and show us the best place to install the ramp. It is curious that a few days following the meeting, a woman called the rectory and asked how our church felt about having a small group of handicapped men attend our Saturday service. She said they sometimes screamed aloud. We talked for quite some time and she was assured that they would be welcomed. So far they haven't come.

How do you convince people that they are indeed welcome? At the meeting, a young professional woman, who worked with special-needs children, spoke at length about environments that were friendly. She explained to us that a person either feels like a place is friendly or they feel it is hostile. While she was talking, it became clear that we needed to find concrete ways of making our church more friendly and more inclusive. Things like our handicapped elevator and handicapped rest rooms were clear messages that the church is friendly. Our new group formed specifically to become more aware of the importance of understanding the special needs of our brothers and sisters with disabilities and life challenges is a direct message of inclusion.

And perhaps that is the best message of all, the opening of our hearts to see and understand "the steps" that exist for many of our brothers and sisters. And, as community, lovingly look for ways to turn those "steps" into "ramps."

Bingo

"Good evening and welcome to St. Blaise Bingo," Ed began, grinning from the pulpit. "That's the way I start each St. Blaise Bingo evening. I'm here to ask you for something very valuable—I'm asking you to volunteer some time—a firm commitment of one Sunday evening a month. We guarantee you will enjoy yourself if you just give it a chance. No experience is necessary, we will train you.

"What are the hours, you ask? 5 p.m. to 10 p.m.—5 hours that really fly by when you're busy selling tickets or specials and talking with the players and other members of the team. We really need you. Some of our old team members have moved, and summer vacations have opened up spots for new members.

"You will tell me that you will not remember which is your week. We have the answer for that. Adele will call you on your week or she will see you in church to give you a gentle reminder.

"Both you and your partner would like to sign up but you have children and don't want to leave them at home alone. No problem! Bingo will pay for the sitter's fee so both husband and wife can have a fun night at Bingo.

"If there are any other concerns, I'm sure we can work them out. So, please see Adele or Ed, that's me, and we'll get you started on making some new friends—having some fun—and doing a good service for the St. Blaise Community. Thank you very much and I'm looking forward to seeing you on a team."

Bingo is one of those words that instantly conjures up a picture.

For us, many pictures easily come to mind, like Adele and the brown suitcase, and Ed: two faithful, tireless people who run bingo. Millie's kitchen and her incomparable hot dogs! Mike, our undefeated salesman. The host of weekly workers like Pat and MaryAnne. Our callers, and all the workers who are part of our monthly teams. Not to mention Father, who needs seven people to replace him if he is absent!

It is only in the past few years that our collections have finally surpassed our bingo revenue. But, we could not pay our bills if it were not for bingo. The poor benefit, too, as our par-

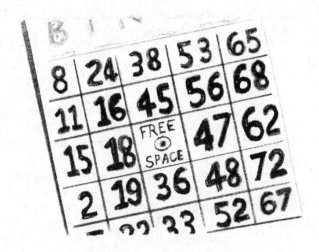

ish tithes from all our income, including bingo. Bingo is not just a source of income, though. The bingo workers have a special relationship with many of the people who come. Bingo has been a channel for people to meet Father, and many people have come to our healing Mass and other services through bingo.

To some, bingo is family. But to us, bingo is a picture of a family working to support itself. On Sunday night the hall is full of people with different needs. Some are waiting for the right number to be called. But for the St. Blaise family who work there, the numbers really don't matter at all.

Holy Stitchers

"Good morning!"

"Good morning, MaryAnne!" the community responded enthusiastically, smiles breaking out in expectation. MaryAnne was always dressed like the way the Fourth of July makes you feel. It was not simply a matter of her clothing. She herself was sparkly and her dark, mischievous brown eyes danced like they knew a secret. Father said that if everyone had a MaryAnne there would be no need for doctors, that's how good she made you feel. Wherever she was, a crowd soon gathered. And in moments, different sounds of laughter would explode in an emotional display of fireworks. She was born on the 4th of July and surely that is the mark of her gift. She captivates you with stories that double you over and before you realize what happened, she has set you free from the worry and tension of the day. It is no wonder ears were perked up to hear what she had to say.

"Well," MaryAnne continued into the mike, "Father said we each had one minute to make our announcements. But I'll take as long as I like." She put her hand on her hip and shot him a winning glance. "What can he do?"

Father leaned his head back and roared with laughter. He seemed to enjoy these intimate moments when we were simply family. Moments that MaryAnne had a natural gift of creating.

"Now that we've got that settled," she continued, "I'll tell you why I'm here. On behalf of the Holy Stitchers, I invite you to join us for a fun-filled evening of crafts and a whole lot of laughs. For those of you who are new to the parish, Holy Stitchers, as Father has dubbed us, is a group of women who gather together to work on craft projects for our annual Fall Family Festival that is held in October. We meet every Monday night downstairs in the church hall. I will attest to the fact that you need not be talented, creative or even good at stitching to join us. After all, I belong." She pointed to herself, gave us her MaryAnne laugh and continued. "But, if you happen to be any of the above-mentioned, you would definitely be most welcomed," she said emphatically.

"At this point, you are probably wondering, what do you do on Monday evening?" She subconsciously glanced over at Father. "And if you were to ask Father, he would tell you that it is one party after another, and on the Monday before the fair we work all night long." She adjusted the mike and proceeded to almost whisper in it, like she was disclosing a secret. "Well, if the truth be known, Father is not too far off the mark. The first part anyway. It is a celebration of sorts. We do have refreshments while we work and share our everyday joys and sorrows, laughter and tears, and then more laughter.

"We got together in the first place because many years ago we used to have an annual bazaar and many of us missed the feeling of community the bazaar brought us. So we decided to start it up again. The Fall Family Festival is a day of games, marvelous food and a raffle with donated handmade items. The raffle gets more spectacular every year. We have sewers, carpenters, painters, artists, quilters, all donating their talents. I never thought we had that many talented people in Bellingham, never mind in our parish!

"So, for all the memories of the past, I thank you. And to all our new parishioners, I welcome you to come on Monday evening to begin to be a part of the making of tomorrow's memories."

She paused and Father began to get up. "I'm not finished yet," she said pointing her finger toward him. "I'll tell you when it's time." Everyone in the church broke up in laughter.

"That Father," she said teasingly. "I just had to tell you one more thing. And this is an added bonus. We never intended for the fair to be a fundraiser. We simply wanted to get together as community. But last year we made $3500.00. How do you like that, and we're not even trying to make money! And like all of our earnings, part of that will be tithed to the poor. Maybe that will be an extra incentive for some. Now I'm finished," she said to Father, stepping off the sanctuary into the middle of the aisle and officially ending the announcement with her trademark—putting her hands together and blowing us a kiss!

The community broke out in spontaneous applause. In a way, the clapping was for all of us: the leaders of all our various ministries, the teachers, discussion leaders, dancers, ushers, music people, Eucharistic Ministers, the lectors, the people who took care of the flowers, the sacristans, the money counters, the bingo workers. The countless people in our church family who had their special tasks that they cheerfully performed for the family, whether it was known or not.

Maybe to God we are like the quilt the "Holy Stitchers" made for the bazaar. Our lives are simple individual pieces of fabric, each with its own color and design. As each piece is added to the whole, the quilt takes on a pattern all its own. We "stitch" our lives together and find, to our surprise, that where many separate pieces used to lie, we now have one very usable quilt. A quilt with no other purpose than to serve the Lord.

Visitation

"Blessed is He who comes in the Name of the Lord!"
John 12:13

She is sometimes concerned about her shaky hands, yet the work she does for the Lord is done with a steady heart. Her soft blue eyes lit up as she told about the Mother's Day card she had received from one of her "children."

Mary retired a short time ago and felt called by the Lord, though she was not quite sure how He would use her. Mary's gentle way with people, her willingness to listen, the great concern that manifests itself from her presence, was an open invitation to do pastoral work. Mary was surprised but very pleased when she was asked if she would be part of the parish visitation ministry. People do not realize how plainly they wear Jesus. Their faces speak the words that are in their hearts, "Let it be done unto me according to your word." They are ready to serve, but oftentimes need a direct invitation to do ministry in the church. Mary enthusiastically said yes to this new calling.

On Thursdays, people watch out their window for that cheerful face who will sit and have a cup of tea. A friend who is never rushed and truly loves each of them as they love her. She is a prayer sent out from the church, a physical prayer that links people to the lifeline of the community, and allows them to receive the Body of Christ.

Father Connolly visits people at home on Tuesdays. He also goes to the nursing homes and hospitals. On Mondays he says a Mass for the residents who are in an adult day care program. On Tuesday morning he goes to an elderly housing complex to say Mass for the residents there. Lianne, who lives at the housing complex, works closely with Father, assisting him at both weekday Masses. She posts all of our newsletters and tithing letters on the bulletin board in the community room. Many people were moved with our outreach to the poor and use envelopes to support what we are doing. Some have found our community through Lianne, who gladly drives them to our Saturday liturgy. She keeps Father informed in a special way about the needs of the elderly where she lives. Besides driving people to get food assistance, she also brings the Eucharist to those who are shut in. Lianne and Mary are there for all the funerals and are part of the Lazarus Ministry as well.

Father has a Jesus way of knowing the needs of the people. He works closely with Mary and Lianne, and directs them to specific people who need visiting. But Father also knows how to get the word out to just the right people in the community who can help specifically in certain situations.

There is a strong network of people in our parish who are part of the visitation ministry, all in unique ways. They are the unseen hands of people like Mary and Alice. They are a ride to the store. They offer a comforting ear. They do errands and truly look after one another.

Father is a channel for the entire parish, especially when people are hurting or sick. It is not uncommon for one member of the parish to drop in and visit another member who is in the hospital, sometimes just for a quick hello during their lunch hour. Mothers who have been sick have related stories of how they didn't have to cook for weeks. Every day someone different dropped off a meal. Or someone knocks on the door to take the children for the day.

These are only a few of the examples that have "leaked out," so to speak. People never mention their quiet work. And surely there are a multitude of others who live out the Beatitudes in their own special way. They too are part of our visitation ministry, messengers who are filled with the Word and bring it into the world.

A woman confided that she had been searching for a church for her family. One Saturday, she had brought her two boys to have muffins with Santa in the basement of our church hall. Before she left, she slipped up the stairs for a moment by herself, and quietly opened the door to the church. A chill went through her entire body. She began to weep uncontrollably. "When I opened the door," she said, "there was Jesus, so warm and real that He touched me."

The church seems to hold our "consecration," the consecration of our lives, the service that is offered to God in those benches. The shared moments of breaking the bread, the spirit, the love among us. And perhaps in the air lingers the sweet voices of our angels, the messengers who reveal and communicate God's presence through their lives. "Blessed is He who comes in the Name of the Lord!"

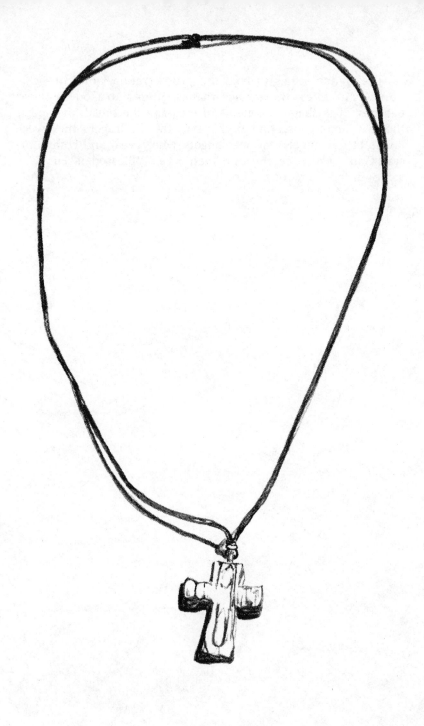

Parish Outreach

"Happy are those who mourn . . ."

Matthew 5:4

Father has firmly implanted in the community the feeling that to mourn is to be moved to action. Our continuing faith development, combined with Father's inspired homilies, move us to look for ways we can be of service in the Kingdom. In fact, we have a new group that was formed in just that spirit, simply to be there in service. They are a motivated group of people of all ages who signed up to be called on in times of need. They will babysit, drive, do errands, virtually fulfill any need that arises.

The St. Blaise cross is visible where people are in need. Members of our parish have plugged into Meals on Wheels. This is a program to bring meals to people who are shut in. Some are part of the Council on Aging. Two wonderful members of our community were like joyous school kids, bringing in boxes of beautiful handmade hats, scarfs and mittens that the seniors had lovingly made for one of our winter projects for the needy.

We have a group who work at Because He Lives, the food kitchen Paul and Pat Dempster started in 1985. For years we had a team from our church who served a meal the last Saturday of the month. Now we have people who wash towels, fold clothes, bring food, and are a link between our parish and the needs of the food kitchen that we, as community, can respond to in addition to our monthly tithe. We have parish members who are part of Hospice. Their cross is a silent evangelizer that often is the channel to open communication about church and Jesus. We have a prison ministry. People in our community who are part of the Scouts and various other town organizations often are the means to lead drives for our food pantry. We have to find ways to let Jesus out of our churches and into the world.

Our church hall and rectory are places where AA, Al-Anon and Narcotics Anonymous hold their meetings during the afternoon, as well as many week nights. Many of the members have met with Father through those meetings. It is our prayer as community that perhaps those in need will one day understand how we have opened our door because of our love for them. And inside those doors await the love and support of an extended family who are happy because they have learned to mourn.

The Lazarus Ministry

"I am telling you the truth: a grain of wheat remains no more than a single grain unless it is dropped into the ground and dies. If it does die, then it produces many grains."

John 12:24

Danny died in the fall of the year, leaving like the bright foliage of autumn, without our permission, with no control, bringing on an early winter. Danny was class president. He was president of the C.Y.O. But more than that, he was a glimpse of Jesus. He was the most popular boy in church, school, work, anywhere he was. Yet he was known for his acceptance of everyone. No one group could claim him; he crossed over all the youth barriers and elevated many who were unaccepted. His friendship made them acceptable.

Danny was outrageous and directed by an inner Spirit that was centered on Jesus. He was 18. Many people remarked what a shame it was that Danny would not make his mark in life, not have a chance to fulfill his purpose. Yet, it became unmistakable to see that his young death was perhaps the greatest mark he could have made. For only through his death did we really see who he was. His dying was the Resurrection for many of his peers. And, as community, we are still witnessing the Resurrection changes that his dying has brought.

Danny's wake and funeral was held at our church. From 6:00 p.m. until 10:30 p.m., more than 2,000 people formed a massive line that rounded the smooth benches of our church from both sides and ended far outside the doors. All during the wake, the folk group played music, including many of Danny's favorite songs. Busy hands directed people to the basement of the church hall for refreshment and comfort. Teenagers were gathered in clusters all through the church, comforting one another, being there as they knew Danny would want them to be. The church was filled to capacity for the funeral, and family and friends were invited back to the church hall for food and nourishment provided and served by the community. The young people lingered until the last possible moment, expressing the community that existed among them.

Danny's wake and funeral was the seed from which the Lazarus Ministry would grow. That shared experience filled us with an awareness of how we wanted and needed to be there for one another as community at that crucial time when a loved one dies.

Wakes used to be in the home, and families performed the last tasks for their loved ones. Gradually this got moved to funeral homes. Today, the family has virtually become bystanders. They are told what to do and how to act at the funeral of their loved one. What once was a part of life has now become regulated by strangers. At the time of death we become almost childlike in that we don't know what to do, so we allow professionals to make our choices for us.

All the important events in our Christian life happen within the context of a community. At First Communion time we hang the pictures up around the church and people sign and drop notes for the children who are making their First Communion. First Communion day is celebrated when we get together as a community.

Confirmation: we pray for the candidates. They make their commitment to the program within the context of the community. They receive the sacrament within the context of the community. Penance: we have within the context of the community. We have our parish penitential celebration. Matrimony: we often have couples renew their marriage vows during our liturgy. We are seeing couples choosing to have their marriage celebrated during one of our liturgies. However, when it comes to death, the community is not there. The time when we Christians believe to be united with Jesus, the fundamental belief of our religion, the community is not there.

How could we, as community, reach out and be there in a meaningful way at the time of death? The answer came through the forming of the Lazarus Ministry.

The members of our Lazarus Ministry are called to be ministers to the bereaved. It is not our intention to take the place of the funeral director. We hope to be able to assist, but only with what the family needs and would find helpful. For a long time we had been allowing professionals to be there for our community members, doing what we felt we should be doing.

Members of the Lazarus Ministry visit the family at home and assist them with the funeral arrangements. They are present to help the family be aware that they can take as active a part in the liturgy as they wish. The family need no longer be bystanders, but can reclaim their right to perform the last tasks for their loved ones.

The family is encouraged to select individuals as pall bearers. They can place the pall on the casket. The family may choose the readings and choose readers of the Word for the liturgy. Members of the family can set the table at the celebration of Eucharist. Family members and/or friends may wish to share some special memories or favorite writings of the deceased. This may be done at meditation. The family has a choice and can select meaningful music for the liturgy. A selection form that offers all of these choices is gone over with the family in detail by a member of the Lazarus Ministry. The completed form is given to the family as a remembrance of the funeral celebration.

One thing we found absolutely necessary was to have direct communication between the Lazarus Ministry and the funeral director. When Ed, a member of our community, volunteered to be the link between the church and the funeral people, there was no longer any confusion as to what services they were expected to perform when it came to the liturgy. We have come to realize the need for the community's presence when the funeral director arrives with the body. We have let strangers take on the care of our loved ones during these times, and it is our intention to be there as community, especially within our own church structure. We will be there as parish family to guide and pray with the dear ones of the deceased, to lead and direct our own liturgies.

Education and dialogue is the key to help people take back this part of life. Gerry, our DRE, is the coordinator for the Lazarus Ministry. Her own experience of death, through the loss of her husband several years ago, has provided insight into the needs of people who are grieving and also an understanding of how families need to approach death. Death was the theme for one of the sessions of our adult religious education program and Gerry was the presenter. Through the adult session, we took a look at how we actually perceive the death experience. It freed families to look at death now, and perhaps begin to make rational decisions about death while everyone is healthy, allowing for rational choices rather than emotional decisions later.

This could be deciding ahead of time the type of casket and answering questions, like whether the most expensive coffin is indeed more meaningful than a simple pine box. We mistakenly think the Big American funeral is the "traditional funeral." Yet from colonial days until the 19th century, the American funeral was almost exclusively a family affair.

Many people talked about feeling a loss of control when it came to making funeral arrangements. They did not have a clear understanding of exactly what they had control over. The program reminded us that we are in charge. We do not have to accept a package, we can buy only the services we want and play as large a role as we wish.

Through the Lazarus Ministry, the community also realized we needed something for people who were grieving. Some of our members have been called to be part of the "Healing Hands." This is our grieving group. When they meet, they deal with feelings that arise when a loved one dies. Grief is a process and those who have been called to this ministry are there to assist the bereaved through this process, which begins with denial and ends with acceptance.

We wish to reach out to all the members of our community. When members of our community have a loved one who dies, we have begun sending cards in the name of our community. These cards have a picture of the loaves and fishes on the outside and inside it states: "A donation has been made to the Loaves and Fishes Food Pantry at St. Blaise in the name of _____."

If there is an absence of the community at the lowest point in our lives, what does this say about our community? The Loaves and Fishes cards enable us to reach the people in our community in a meaningful way. It is a connection to community.

Another wonderful connection came with our Book of Remembrance. Last October the Book of Remembrance was placed on the side altar. Everyone in the parish could write down the name of a loved one they wanted remembered. When we had our special liturgy on All Soul's Day, this book was placed on the altar as part of the offertory. The community also sent out an invitation to the families of the people who had died that year, who were members of our community. The invitation read:

> You are invited to a special Liturgy, November 2 at 7:00 p.m., in remembrance of those members of our community who have passed away during this year. You are also invited to participate in a special meditation during this liturgy. At meditation these, our newly resurrected, will be named and Father will light a candle for them. At this time a member of their family, or someone of the family's choosing, is invited to receive the candle. If it is not possible for your family to respond to this invitation, a member of our Lazarus Ministry will come forward to receive the candle and will make sure it is passed on to your family. We hope you will be able to be with us to whatever degree of participation you feel comfortable with. We hope you will join us for coffee in the church hall afterwards.

The response was wonderful. All but three families came. They felt that the community cared about them. They felt a closeness with the people who died. As the bell was rung for each name and the family came up to receive the light, you could feel the presence of their Spirit in the church. The grieving felt connected to their deceased loved one. This was a connection that they needed to have—emotionally they are feeling this anyway, but now they were able to spiritually and physically (symbolically through the candle which they were given to take home—the Body of Christ—a reminder, too, that we are together as one body) feel the connection.

We need meaningful rituals and signs like the candles and the bell intoning that will reach into the emotional level where people live. We need rituals that do this so we can move beyond and resolve any relationships that need healing.

Almost everyone came downstairs for coffee and cake. Many parishioners from our community had called and driven people to the Mass who are elderly or do not drive at night. The time in the hall was a shared moment of community. People didn't want to let go of the connection. They felt they were One Body. They needed to meet socially to ease back into the world. They felt safe, cared for, joined to the loved one, understood, and allowed to have this feeling of grief accepted as real.

We are no longer bystanders at the time of death. The funeral directors bring the body into the church. But from that point on, the professionals leave, and the family, the church family, is there to guide and pray with the dear ones of the deceased. We are there to welcome them into our community through the sacrament of Baptism, and now we stand in consolation and strength as a family, watching as the cycle of our faith in Jesus is completed, victory over death as we share in the resurrection.

Strains of music Brian wrote and sang for meditation at our Remembrance liturgy fill the air of our church as strongly as the incense we burn. "They're only now as far away as faith keeps them from you, and only those with eyes to see will know these words are true."

Danny, "our" Danny, still bounces through the church in his disconcerted outfit, half Hawaiian, half CYO. His smile, that always started in those sparkling blue eyes, is still changing lives. He did his Father's will and surely made him smile, because Danny's smile was always contagious. And we, who are forever joined by faith, share in that smile through the little pine tree that the CYO planted in Danny's memory: a precious reminder that life continues on even after the earliest of winters.

The Wedding

"Wherever you go, I will go; wherever you live, I will live. Your people will be my people, and your God will be my God."

Book of Ruth

"Anne and Gary will receive many treasured gifts today, but the greatest of these is the gift of your presence—the gift of family. The St. Blaise Community is Anne and Gary's church family. We warmly welcome you to our liturgy where we will celebrate the wedding of Anne and Gary. We, too, feel enriched by your presence."

So began the 10:00 liturgy on Sunday, the 12th of July, 1992. But it had all really started earlier that morning when the dew was still clinging to the freshly-cut lawn. Family after family arrived to transform the churchgrounds for the reception that would immediately follow the Mass. Chairs had been strategically scattered in friendly clusters in and about the graceful trees and shrubs that formed Father's lovely bird sanctuary. Tables were decorated with white cloths and fresh flowers. The trees were dressed in streamers and bells to celebrate the occasion. Three long tables edged the side of the church walkway, eagerly awaiting the fresh-brewed coffee, cold juices, and delightful breakfast treats that were planned for the guests. And for the background, God chose a perfect blue sky and all the brilliance of a summer day.

The church was clothed in Father's vision of parish, his vision of the Kingdom: a community simply loving one another, being there for one another in every time of celebration. Anne said she could not find tasks for all the people who had personally offered to help in any way they could. The community provided the reception. The music people, both the folk group and the organist, were there with their gifts of music. Anne's friends from the bell choir had come to perform. And the liturgical dancers were eager to return their gift of dance to Anne, their beloved teacher, who had given them the gift of dancing for the Lord.

Too quickly, Anne and Gary were seated for the meditation. The dancers were holding their breath, waiting for the sound of that first note that would grant their feet permission to step out onto the sanctuary. Anne was dressed in the wedding gown her grandmother wore 65 years ago. The delicate features of her young face took on the blush of a bride. And as she sat so radiantly beneath the Resurrected Lord, she looked as much the bride of Jesus as she did the bride of Gary, something of which his sensitive boyish features seemed well aware. Suddenly the music filled the heart of the church as the young people, her "children," floated out behind the altar.

It was their idea to dance for her, and how shyly they had asked. Now the dance radiated all the love they felt and her eyes, her very soul, joined them in the dance. Anne led them out at the close of the liturgy, taking their hands in an unbroken chain, to be joined by row after row of people in the benches.

This joyful gathering of friends and family spilled out onto the lawns, as in a postcard scene that suddenly became real. How delighted Anne was to ride in her surprise gift from her "children," a horse and buggy that was gracefully driven to circle the church grounds.

Family and church family mingled, the conversation inevitably turning to church at some point. Many shared their pleasant surprise and joy at what they discovered that morning. Some hadn't been to church for a while. As the buggy circled round and round the churchgrounds, each time picking up and dropping off new faces, stories also circled, stories they remembered when the church bell still rang on Sunday.

Anne and Gary finally said their goodbyes. Guests began to follow their lead. Slowly, people began to clean up. The tables were broken down, chairs were carried to the church hall. The children were begging for one last ride. A family lingered under the shade of a tree, saying their farewell, trying to hold on to the moment. Tomorrow they were moving away.

As people walked to their cars, only the majestic copper beech tree heard the conversations that continued, and revealed the feelings of the morning. But as they passed the little Lighthouse that stood like a sentry, some would be surprised to hear a voice whisper, "Bring my sons from afar and my daughters from the ends of the earth. Come, this is the way home."

Epilogue

*"The light shines in the darkness,
and the darkness has never put it out."*

John 1:5

There was a small fishing village along the coast where people grew up accepting certain things simply because that was the way they were taught and it had become a way of life for them. They often told one another, "There's nothing I can do." They were people of the sea.

Everyone knew that if one of the boats didn't make it home before a storm hit, they were certain to find destruction in the morning. All the families would gather at the shore to pick up the shattered pieces that floated in. They looked at the vastness of the sea, felt powerless against her might, and offered a silent prayer that they wouldn't be next. For there seemed to be more and more boats crashing every month. They encouraged one another the best way they knew how, by all agreeing that there was really nothing anyone could do.

One night a storm hit that was worse than any of them had known. The night was totally without light. The rain drove so hard against the roof that no other sound was heard. And although smoke rose from the chimneys of all the weathered cottages, there was no warmth to be taken from the fire. One of the boats had not made it in.

Just then a violent burst of thunder shook the night and for a brief moment a flash of lightning lit the sky. Without a word, a man jumped to his feet, grabbed his sea gear, and running out into the stormy night, simply called to his family, "No time to explain now." They pressed their faces against the windowpane and watched as he disappeared into the shed. Suddenly, in the dark night, they saw his lantern swinging by his side as he

167

headed down to the seacoast. He walked out of their sight but somehow the darkness could not succeed in swallowing the light.

All through the long hours of the night, he stood on the shore and guided the boat safely away from the dangerous rocks along the coast. It didn't take long for word to spread that the boat had survived the storm. The people ran from their cottages to see what possibly could have had the power to make a difference.

And there on the dangerous, rocky shore stood one person with one small light.

Even the Best Lights Need Tending

Brian and Phyllis are available to share their Ministry with your parish. The Lighthouse Ministry provides an evening of stories and song that allow for a non-threatening way to share with parents the difference church makes in the family. Stories that remind us of our relationship with Jesus. And deep down parents understand that only through the experience of church in the family can our children have this same relationship with the Lord.

Brian and Phyllis have two children, ages 22 and 20; both are in college. Yet, they realize the greatest gift they have given them is not an education, but the precious gift of Jesus and the church. That is their message.

Parents need to be aware that they indeed are the first teachers in the ways of faith. Their own faith commitment will be their children's faith foundation. And humbly, Brian and Phyllis find Jesus using the Lighthouse Ministry for this purpose. For parents who are firmly rooted in parish life, their presentation encourages and reaffirms the importance of their commitment to church. For parents who are not so connected, their ministry rekindles the light of their faith. The Lighthouse is a beautiful, gentle reminder that Jesus is the Light and that we are called to be Keepers of the Light.

To schedule an evening with the Lighthouse Ministry, write to:

> The Lighthouse Ministry
> 15 Andrew Street
> Bellingham, MA 02019
>
> or call: (508) 883-4083